Understand
Those
Feelings

UNDERSTAND THOSE FEELINGS

EUGENE T.
McDONALD

STANWIX HOUSE, INC.
Pittsburgh

Published simultaneously in Canada by
The House of Grant (Canada) Ltd.
Toronto, Ontario

First printing - March 1962
Second printing - September 1963

Library of Congress catalog card number
61—18740

To Patty Anne
whose short life will be long remembered
for the many lessons it helped us learn.

About the Author

The author, Eugene T. McDonald, is director of the Speech and Hearing Clinic at The Pennsylvania State University in University Park, Pennsylvania. Dr. McDonald has worked with handicapped children and their parents in public schools, juvenile courts, hospital clinics, treatment centers operated by crippled children's societies, residential schools for handicapped children, and at his University office. He also serves on the advisory boards of several local, state, and national organizations which are interested in problems of handicapped children and adults.

Dr. McDonald is a Fellow of the American Psychological Association, a Fellow of the American Speech and Hearing Association, and a member of the American Academy for Cerebral Palsy. He is a past-president of the American Association for Cleft Palate Rehabilitation and a former editor of The Cleft Palate Bulletin.

His participation in many post-doctoral training programs and his long affiliation with several teams of rehabilitation specialists have given Dr. McDonald a broad, multi-disciplinary approach to rehabilitation problems. Ed. Note.

Contents

Chapter I - A POINT OF VIEW 1

The feelings of parents should be of as much concern to professional workers as the diagnosis and treatment of the child's problem. When parents have an opportunity to talk in a friendly, unhurried manner with counselors, they speak of their embarrassments, hostilities, suspicions, and other troubled feelings. While the details differ from family to family, many of the feelings discussed by parents are similar regardless of the nature of the child's handicap. These feelings have very natural and simple origins. When these origins and developmental patterns are understood, the feelings may be effectively directed and controlled. When parents don't understand the naturalness of their feelings, the feelings often develop in unwholesome directions. Often appropriate information, proper guidance, a positive action program, and TIME are all a family needs to develop the feelings which lead to peace of mind.

Chapter II - LEARNING SOMETHING IS WRONG 7

Parents learn that something is wrong with their child either by someone telling them or through their own observation of their child's failure to develop normally. The period between the time when parents learn that something is wrong and the time when they learn what can be done about it is a very trying period. With many unanswered questions parents become confused. Unrecognized and unmanaged feelings of confusion lead to feelings of insecurity and anxiety. Effective antidotes to confusion are: appropriate and accurate information obtained when needed and when parents are ready for it; organization of thoughts and feelings; participation in a positive action program; and TIME. Ill feelings sometimes naturally arise toward the professional person who first reports a child's handicapping condition to the parents. These feelings lead to rejection of the diagnosis and parental "shopping" for a more optimistic evaluation. Understanding of the basis of one's feelings toward the doctor or other professional worker who first explained that something was wrong with the child can prevent the additional confusion which arises from "shopping."

Chapter III - UNFULFILLED EXPECTATIONS 23

Parents look forward to having a child who will walk like other children, talk like other children, go to school, get a job, get married—do all the things other people do. When it becomes apparent that because of some handicapping condition of the child these expectations can at best be only partially realized, disappointment naturally sets in. Deep and long-lasting disappointment can adversely influence the parents' relationships with the handicapped child by creating psychological barriers between parent and child. Feelings of disappointment may be counteracted by: learning that disappointment is a natural reaction to unfulfilled expectations; changing expectations; thinking of the child's capabilities as well as his liabilities; becoming involved in a positive action program. Parents of handicapped children may never completely get over their disappointment but they can learn to understand and lessen this feeling.

Chapter IV - WHAT WILL PEOPLE THINK? 33

Our need to be accepted by others is an important motivating force in our lives. Parents of handicapped children sometimes feel that relatives and friends, in fact, the public in general, do not accept them nor their handicapped child. Sometimes this feeling is warranted because there are some people who don't feel comfortable with handicapped persons. Usually, though, people are more accepting than parents realize. When acceptance is withheld it is often because of the attitudes of the parents themselves. Parental reticence to discuss their child's problem, forcing themselves into situations and demanding acceptance are among the factors which interfere with gaining acceptance. Some ways in which parents can make themselves and their handicapped children more acceptable are: understand the need for acceptance; recognize that some people find it difficult to accept anyone who is different; become aware that most people are more accepting than you might expect; be willing to discuss their child's problem honestly when occasion arises; learn that the feelings of others are often a reflection of our own feelings; increase their child's acceptability.

Sometimes problems arise because people are too accepting.

Parents of handicapped children may meet these problems by: recognizing that some people are sincere in their desire to be of help and avoid rebuffing them; understanding the nature of their reactions to people who offer assistance; learning what kind of help they can use; trying to redirect the efforts of persons who want to help to their best advantage or to the best advantage of handicapped people in general.

Chapter V - THOSE FLUSTERED FEELINGS 55

Embarrassment occurs naturally anytime attention, either favorable or unfavorable, is focused on us. Most embarrassment is of short duration but that associated with having a handicapped child may be long lasting. The basically simple reaction of embarrassment can become quite complex and give rise to feelings of anger and hostility. Such strong feelings, when not recognized and understood, rarely remain compartmentalized but may spread to influence parental reactions to professional workers as well as to others with whom the parents come into contact. Some suggestions developed in parent group discussions for handling embarrassment are: learn to recognize embarrassment and how it affects behavior; recognize that most people are curious; become aware that some embarrassing situations may be of one's own making; operate on the philosophy that parents of handicapped children should function as public relations representatives for all handicapped persons. Following these suggestions will not mean that one will never be embarrassed again but attention to these suggestions will reduce the number of times embarrassing incidents arise relating to one's handicapped child and will help prevent embarrassment from developing into anger and hostility.

Chapter VI - WHO'S TO BLAME? 65

Man has always tried to explain to himself why things happen as they do and it is natural for him to try to explain things on the basis of his experience using the information he has at hand. Since parents usually don't have scientific information about the causes of handicapping conditions, they naturally attribute their problem to some supernatural forces.

Everyone can recall some wrongdoings of his past and parents of handicapped children often guiltily conclude that having a handicapped child is a punishment for their sins. As parents come to understand the nature of their children's conditions and learn that scientific investigations have shed much light on the cause of these problems, they recognize the inadequacy of self-incriminating explanations. Sometimes parents feel that they have done something which is directly responsible for their child's problem. Others may ascribe their child's handicap to a doctor's negligence or incompetence. Concern about placing the blame on someone can adversely color much of a parent's feeling about his child and the professional workers who are trying to be of help.

Parents have learned to handle this feeling by: changing the question from "Who is to blame?" to "What might have caused it?"; discovering as much as possible what science has learned about the condition; discussing fully with a trusted professional worker their thoughts about possible causes. Occasionally professional workers will unwittingly arouse guilt feelings in self-critical parents. Frank inquiries about potentially disturbing matters will result in better mental hygiene for parents and the improved inter-communication will help the professionals increase their effectiveness.

Chapter VII - WORRY, WORRY, WORRY 85

From the dawn of history man has been concerned about the question—"What of the future?"—and much of his activity is directed toward the development of many kinds of devices and programs which will protect his security. Natural concern about how their children will spend their future lives is the seed from which much parental worry and anxiety develop. When the child's future is darkened by a disability, parental concern quickly takes on the emotional overtones characteristic of chronic worry. Parents of children who cannot become sufficiently independent to take care of themselves are constantly tormented by the question—"Who will take care of our child after we're gone?"

A parent group offered these criteria for developing or selecting a future care program for severely disabled children:

provide care adequate to meet the child's needs; afford an opportunity to live in dignity; guaranteed continuity of care; cost not to exceed parents' ability to pay. There are many other sources of worry for parents of handicapped children, such as their natural desire to protect their children from hurt and pain. Parent groups have identified these four steps in learning to manage one's worry about a handicapped child: recognize that worry is a natural reaction; learn to identify the cause of worry; work to eliminate the cause of worry; recognize that all worry cannot be eliminated. Worry and anxiety are common reactions of men. Probably no man can ever rid himself of them. Nor is this desirable. A more desirable goal would be to eliminate those worries for which the causes can be removed and to minimize worries for which the cause is not removable.

Chapter VIII - CHILDREN HAVE TWO PARENTS . . . 118

Many parents of handicapped children have thought all their marital difficulties were traceable to their having a handicapped child. Having a handicapped child does create special strains on a marital relationship because of the extra demands on time, energy, family income, and the inevitable influences a handicapped child has on parental attitudes and feelings. However, there are many forces operating in our society today which produce serious marital discord and it is unlikely that the handicapped child is the sole source of his parents' marital problems. Having a handicapped child calls for stronger efforts on the part of both parents to adjust to this as well as to the many other problems of married life. Many parents have learned to ease the natural marital frictions associated with parenthood of a handicapped child by: recognizing that some disagreements are inevitable in marriage; recognizing that the pursuit of marital happiness is a lifelong obligation; sharing the work; learning how to talk together about their problems. Too frequently, even when his parents continue to live together, the handicapped child has, in effect, only a one-parent family. Parental understanding of the forces which lead to this unhappy family situation can help the handicapped child enjoy the advantages of having two parents. It can help the parents enjoy their lives more fully also.

Chapter IX - FAITH OF THEIR FATHERS 137

Freedom to worship as we wish is cherished by our people and guaranteed by the first amendment to the Constitution. One's right to believe as he wishes is undeniable—so long as his beliefs don't give him license to violate the rights of others. In a democracy the right of a handicapped person to receive habilitation services is also inalienable. Only by closing their eyes to the injustice they are doing can parents find peace of mind while denying habilitation services to their handicapped child on the basis of religious beliefs. While some parents want to turn their problems over to God, others denounce God for letting their child be handicapped. The Biblical text, "He maketh His sun to rise on the evil and on the good, and sendeth rain on the just and on the unjust," suggests that this is a world of law and order, where all people are subject to cause and effect. Many parents are helped by the thought that the hand of God is behind the laws and order of nature and that He has given man the intelligence to discover the laws and understand the order. Handicapping conditions arise because of man's failure to understand nature's laws. Their belief that, in our time, God works through man has provided spiritual strength for many parents. Those parents who pray for the wisdom to understand and the strength to accept their handicapped children's problems seem to open their minds to receive information about their children and they seem to grow stronger in their ability to accept the difficulties they and their handicapped children must face.

Chapter X - THOSE PROFESSIONAL PEOPLE 157

There is in many of us a latent hostility toward professional people. Our natural reaction to bearers of ill tidings is resentment. One cannot help but feel some annoyance at being kept waiting, receiving less time than one would like, or getting what appear to be short answers to one's questions. For these, and other reasons, parents of handicapped children very naturally have some hostility toward professionals lying dormant, ready to spring to life on the slightest provocation. Often professional workers, especially doctors, can't predict exactly how much time they must spend with a patient; hence, some people are unavoidably forced to wait. Even when they appear to be hurrying, most professional workers are learning enough about the problem to know what to do next. Sometimes professional workers will knowingly run the risk of leaving parents dissatisfied with the amount of information given rather than create anxiety by giving parents information for which they are not yet ready. Parents of handicapped children get their image of professional workers from their own personal contacts with professional workers, comments of other people, and from stories in newspapers and magazines or on television. Professional workers are highly trained persons devoted to serving their fellow man to the best of their ability. Many factors operate to obscure this image. Parental understanding of these factors can improve their relationships with professional workers.

Chapter XI - A POSITIVE ACTION PROGRAM 177

Participation in a two-level positive action program affords many parents of handicapped children an effective antidote for their troubled feelings. The first level is a personal level at which parents do everything they can to meet all the needs of their handicapped child and to work through their own problems. At the second level parents work to implement the philosophy that every handicapped person, regardless of the type of handicapping condition, age, race, or creed is entitled to all the rehabilitation services which are required to meet his needs and which will lead to a maximum utilization of his potentials. Parents should work to ensure that the nature and extent of the program their community develops for its handicapped will be determined by the needs of the handicapped persons living in the community rather than by the desire of the citizen to be of help. Learning to understand the nature and developmental patterns of their feelings and attitudes, laboring diligently to provide the services their children need, and working conscientiously in the interest of all handicapped persons will not make all the problems of parents of handicapped children disappear for no one can expect to get rid of all his problems. We can, however, learn to live more effectively with them.

Preface

In a real sense this book has been written by many people—
the parents of handicapped children who speak through the
author. Associates who have read the manuscript have asked,
"Are the quotations actually based on what parents have
said?" To this, the answer is Yes. Then they ask, "Are these
the actual words of the parents?" To this question, the answer
is, "Sometimes yes and sometimes no." Often the discussions
are recreations rather than verbatim reports.

During many years of talking with parents of handicapped
children and with parents of non-handicapped children the
topics considered in this book have been discussed many times.

As a result of these discussions the author has noted four important points about the feelings of parents whose children are handicapped:

1. Many problems are shared by all parents of handicapped children regardless of the type of handicap.

2. Most of these problems have their origin in natural, everyday reactions and become serious only when misunderstood and misdirected.

3. Unless feelings are understood and properly directed, handicapped families tend to develop around handicapped children.

4. Most parents can work through their own problems if given proper guidance.

It is to be expected that different groups of parents, in fact, even different individual parents, will make similar comments because of their commonality of problem and feeling. By themselves, however, these comments often do not solve a problem or help one understand and control his feelings. Only when the comments are organized around a central problem do their full meaning and import become clear. This responsibility for organizing and interpreting has been my task when serving as a discussion leader for groups of parents of handicapped children. It is also my task in this book. Around the questions and problems which are shared by most parents of handicapped children, I have pulled together the comments parents have made when these questions and problems have been discussed. While I have tried to maintain the general tone of parents' comments I have often paraphrased their remarks in order to make a point more sharply. Many comments are quoted vertabim.

Friends have asked if I ever have to fabricate a story to make or illustrate a point. The fact that fabrication is rarely necessary is strong testimony to the emotional and intellectual resourcefulness parents can bring to the solution of their own problems. It is the author's hope that this book will help parents of handicapped children learn how to tap and develop their own emotional and intellectual resources so they can understand and control their feelings.

The author wants to express his appreciation to the many parents who have allowed him to share their problems and in that way made this book possible. To the staff members of the treatment centers where these parents have been seen, thanks are due for help in thinking through the problems of parents of handicapped children and for their efforts in helping parents understand and manage their feelings. The author is also appreciative of the opportunities to discuss problems of handicapped children and their parents with Walter and Marguerite Matheny of the Walter D. Matheny School for Cerebral Palsied Children in Peapack, New Jersey. While many colleagues have contributed to the development of concepts presented in this book, special acknowledgment must be made of the professional stimulation of Dr. Burton Chance who has generously shared with the author what he has learned about handicapped children through his vast experience as Medical Director of the Home of the Merciful Saviour for Crippled Children in Philadelphia and as a consultant to many treatment programs.

The comments from John R. Whitney, Rector, St. Andrews Episcopal Church, State College, Pennsylvania, and John D. Walmer, M.D., Psychiatrist, Health Center, The Pennsylvania State University, were most helpful to the author in preparing the manuscript.

By his continuing demonstration that the busy clinician can

contribute regularly to the advancement of professional knowledge, Dr. Meyer Perlstein motivated the author to make and record the observations which constitute the basis of this book. For this inspiration and the knowledge gained while working with Dr. Perlstein, the author expresses his gratitude. To Beverly Solomon the author owes special thanks for the inspiration he has derived from observing her success in living a happy, useful life despite a serious physical handicap and for her thoughtful comments about this manuscript.

Grateful acknowledgment is made to the following publishers for permission to quote from their publications:

The Story of Mankind, Hendrik Willem van Loon, Black and Gold Library, Liveright Publishers, New York. Copyright (R) 1948 by Helen C. van Loon.

Why Did This Have to Happen to Me? John D. Lee, Copyright 1957 by Forward Movement Publications, Cincinnati.

Building an Estate for a Crippled Child, George M. Rideout and John D. Riordan, Copyright 1959 by the National Society for Crippled Children and Adults, Chicago.

Why Do Good People Suffer? Robert R. Youngs, Copyright by The Laymen's Movement for a Christian World, Rye, New York. Published in the September 1959 issue of *The Reader's Digest.*

Eugene T. McDonald

State College, Pennsylvania
October, 1961

Why?

A child came by
        With body frail;
We ask God why
        He sends travail.
Why bind a child
        To life so scant?
Petitions filed,
        He does not grant.
Why parents hurt,
        Nor let them find
Ways to avert
        A troubled mind?

The answer comes,
        But long it takes;
Time's depths it plumbs,
        And sense it makes.
Cause and effect —
        Laws man must know,
If we expect
        To end such woe.

Man's groping mind
        Is slow to learn,
But laws he'll find,
        And mind's peace earn.

                        E. T. M.

I

A Point of View

About 20 years ago, while I was working as a psychologist for two rural counties, a school superintendent asked me to make an evaluation of a 10-year-old boy who seemed unable to profit from school and whose behavior usually kept his class in a turmoil. From the school history it appeared that this boy would prove to be severely mentally retarded. Thinking that it might make it easier to explain his problem to the father, I invited him to observe my testing of the boy. He sat quietly throughout the test but as soon as I was finished, he demanded, "Well, how did he do? What's going to happen now?" I started to explain that the boy's level of mental development was not high enough to enable him to profit from school attendance. The father, a businessman, interrupted, "You s. o. b., these little tricks you use don't tell you anything. You'd starve to death if you had to earn a living in business." Annoyed, I allowed that perhaps he was right but I would still have to recommend that his son be excluded from school. After casting further aspersions on my professional competence and my ancestry, the father avowed that he would enter his son in a neighboring school district where he also owned property. With a motivation that was probably more personal than professional, I explained that I was also the psychologist for that district and that the same school laws pertained in both places. Finally he left, unconvinced of his child's limitations, and hostile toward the schools and everyone associated with them. I thought to myself, "There goes a mean customer who probably deserves all the trouble he has."

About a year ago I received a letter from a father asking me to examine his 5-year-old son who didn't talk. In the letter the father warned that he would punch in the nose anyone who intimated that his son was mentally retarded. Early in our evaluation of the boy it became clear that severe mental retardation was the major cause of the retarded speech development. This was explained to the parents and, as the conference drew to a close, the father got up from his chair, walked over to my desk, stuck out his hand, and thanked me for helping him understand his son and himself better.

Why did these two conferences end so differently? Was it just that the parents were different kinds of people? Partly, I suppose, but more importantly, as a result of talking with several hundred parents whose children were crippled, blind, deaf, mentally retarded, cerebral palsied, or speech defective, I had learned that the psychologist should be as much concerned with the feelings of parents as he was with the diagnosis of the child's problem. I had learned that often the entire family—not just the handicapped child—needed help.

It has often been helpful to parents to learn how these changes in my thinking and in my approach came about. After I have spoken with parent groups about my professional experience in counseling parents, some have commented that they now had a better idea of what kind of help to expect from counselors. When I first began practicing as a psychologist I held the point of view that my responsibility was to find out what was wrong with the child, report this to the parents, and tell them what to do about it. Had I worked only in a diagnostic clinic where parents were seen but once I might have followed this procedure for years without becoming aware that often this approach is ineffective and sometimes harmful.

At the University Clinic where I worked I would interview the parents, make various tests and observations of the child, describe his problem as I saw it to the parents, tell them what to do, and then bid them good-bye, usually never to see them again. As I became aware that often the parents had been to other clinics where the same diagnosis and recommendations had been made, I grew to feel that something important must be missing from our approach. Something often prevented the parents from accepting the diagnosis and carrying out the recommendations.

In addition to being the Director of a University Speech and Hearing Clinic, I have had the fortunate experience of serving as a consultant for several treatment centers for crippled children. In this capacity I have talked regularly with the same families over a period of several years. When a diagnostic program is associated with a treatment center the professional staff has to live with its diagnoses and recommendations. Frequently the treatment staff has opportunities to observe how parents react to the information and advice given them by

medical and other professional specialists. Through periodic
conferences with members of the treatment staff and with the
parents I came to realize that the problems of a family with a
handicapped child might be compared to an iceberg. Only a
small fraction of an iceberg projects above the surface of the
water where it may be seen. The larger part, and often more
dangerous, lies hidden from view, submerged beneath the surface. And so it is with the problems of handicapped children
and their families. The part of the problem which is seen when
a specialist examines or evaluates the child is often small in
comparison to the way the family feels about the problem. The
depth of the parents' anxiety cannot be gauged by studying
the child alone. Yet, these submerged feelings can be as important in the habilitation of a child as the extent of his physical
condition.

Parent Feelings Are Similar

To learn about these feelings I encouraged parents to talk to
me. Casually I would ask, "When did you first notice that Mary
didn't seem to be doing well?" Or, "How did you first learn that
Billy had something wrong with his palate?" From such questions it became apparent that much emotional trauma is often
associated with the manner in which parents first became
aware that something was wrong with their child. Another casual comment and question—"I suppose you have often wondered about what caused it. What are some of the causes
you've thought about?"—showed that many parents were deeply concerned about the cause of their child's problem. When
not helped to think things through they sometimes needlessly
blamed themselves or dreamed up fantastic causes which affected their feelings. The questions—"What are you most concerned about now? Is there anything you'd like to talk

about?"—often brought forth expressions of concern about what the future held for the child. When discussions were held in a friendly, unhurried manner, parents spoke of their embarrassments, hostilities, suspicions, and other troubled feelings.

From these many conferences with individual families it became clear that while the details differ from family to family many of the problems are similar regardless of the nature of the child's handicap. This similarity showed up even more sharply when we began counseling parents in groups of ten or twelve. In these meetings where parents were encouraged to speak freely with only occasional comment from the discussion leader, every doubt, fear, or concern expressed by one parent had been experienced by others in the group. As I became skilled in making the atmosphere of the parent conferences more friendly, accepting, and helpful, parents talked more freely about the questions and feelings they had long kept stored up within them. Judging from the comments of the thousand or so parents with whom I have talked, a family cannot have a handicapped child without developing some troubled feelings about the situation. Since a child does not exist in isolation but as part of a family it is not enough to treat the child's problem and disregard the family's feelings. In a very real sense we never have just a handicapped child, but rather a handicapped family. To be maximally effective, a treatment program should regard the family as the patient and provide not just treatment for the child but also a program designed to help parents understand and manage their feelings.

Problems Begin as Natural Reactions

The feelings of parents of handicapped children have very natural origins. Everyone, whether the parent of a handicapped child or not, at one time or another becomes confused, is disappointed, is embarrassed, etc. Of course, when such feelings are related to a handicapped child they go much deeper but the nature of their beginnings is similar. When parents don't understand this naturalness of their feelings, the feelings may develop in unwholesome directions.

Direction of Feelings May Be Guided

It is the purpose of this book to describe some of the feelings which are common to parents of handicapped children, show how such feelings begin, and tell about some ways in which parents have effectively managed their feelings. The material in this book is based on several hundred conferences with parents. A few of these families were seen but once, many of them have been seen periodically over a period of several years, and some have been seen in small groups which meet about once a week for six sessions. No attempt is made to present a deep psychological evaluation of the parents' comments or feelings. While, obviously, some parents of handicapped children may have adjustment problems arising from personal immaturity, religious differences, socio-economic problems, etc., these are not our concern in this book. Our interest is in those feelings which develop directly from the fact that there is a handicapped child in the family. These feelings, while serious, are usually not of the sort for which deep counseling or psychotherapy is required. Often appropriate information, proper guidance, a positive action program, and *time* are all a family needs to develop the feelings which lead to peace of mind.

II

Learning Something
Is Wrong

There are two common ways in which parents first learn that
something is wrong with their child. Either someone tells them,
or the parents themselves gradually come to the conclusion
that something is wrong after observing their child's failure to
develop normally. Either way, the parents are in for a trying
period. As one older father put it, "During the time between
when I learned that something was wrong with my child and
when I learned what could be done about it I went through
hell." He went on to say that the most disturbing period of his
entire life was that period when he knew something was wrong
but didn't yet know what to do about it.

When a child's defect is obvious at birth the doctor usually
tells the father if he is available. The father, then, is often left
with the responsibility of explaining the child's difficulty to his

wife. The upsetting effect of suddenly learning that something is wrong is vividly illustrated by the report of a father who told how, after the doctor told him his baby had a cleft palate, he had walked the street "the rest of that night, all next day and far into the next night." He said that as he wandered around he was wondering what a cleft palate was, how he could tell his wife that their baby wasn't normal, and where he'd get the money for the child's care. He said, "The thoughts just kept milling around in my mind. I wondered why this had to happen to us and what my wife's parents and the neighbors would think. After awhile I got to wondering what the baby would look like and if he would be okay like the doctor said."

A mother whose boy was born with a congenital amputation of the leg and a deformed right arm said that, even though the doctor and her husband had told her about the baby's malformations and assured her everything would be all right, she was "horrified" when she first saw her son. "How can he ever walk or learn to write?" she worried. Telling a group about her feelings she said that in the weeks following Sammy's birth she was "tortured by dozens of questions." She said she worried about whether he *really* could walk with an artificial leg; what would one cost? "Would other children make fun of Sam or want to play with him? Won't people think I am a bad mother to have produced only part of a child?" As the group listened she kept pouring out questions and then ended, "I seemed to be thinking of all these questions at the same time. I just couldn't get my thoughts organized. My thoughts were all jumbled!"

It is not just the tension and anxiety associated with going to a hospital and waiting through the period of labor for the delivery of a baby which causes parents to have these mixed-up feelings when they are told something is wrong with their child. Anytime parents are suddenly or unexpectedly informed that their child is in some way different from normal children these reactions are to be expected. The following dialogue is based on a conference I had with a young mother who, in her inexperience, had noticed nothing unusual about her child when she took her to a doctor for a six-month checkup.

"When the doctor told me Lynn had cerebral palsy and was probably mentally retarded, too, the bottom just dropped out of everything!" The woman speaking was the mother of 5-year-old Lynn. I had just asked her how she had learned that something was wrong with the way Lynn was developing.

"Do you remember what you thought about at the time?" I inquired.

"At first I couldn't think at all and then I began to think of everything all at once," she replied. "My thoughts were all mixed-up and I just got more and more confused."

"What were some of the thoughts that came into your mind?" I asked.

"I kept wondering," said Lynn's mother, "'Is the doctor right? What could have caused it? How will I tell her father? Will she ever walk? What will our relatives think? Is there anything we can do about it?'—and a million other things, I guess."

Unanswered Questions Beget Confusion

Common to all these experiences are two factors. First, each parent reported having many questions and, second, the parents did not have the answers to their questions. When these two factors are present, confusion is inevitable.

Everyone at one time or another experiences the feeling of

bewilderment which comes from having too many unanswered questions. When I have to drive in an unfamiliar part of a large city I often feel a degree of confusion. Not knowing exactly where I am going I ask myself, "How far down is Blank street? Will I have to turn right or left? I wonder if I can make a left turn at Blank street? What if it's one-way? What lane should I be in?" If the traffic is heavy my confusion is greater, especially if its speed forces me to make decisions quickly. Obviously this confusion is very superficial compared with the confusion experienced upon learning that something is wrong with a child, yet, the genesis of this confusion, like that of the parents, lies in having too many unanswered questions.

One day I found my 12-year-old daughter staring into space with a bewildered look on her face. In response to my question—"What's the matter, Sis?"—she replied, "I have so many things to do . . . !"

"Why don't you get started on them instead of just sitting there?" I suggested.

"I can't," she replied. "I have so much to do I don't know where to start."

Here we see it again—a mild sort of confusion growing out of having too many things to think about and to do all at once.

Have you ever tried to read an insurance policy? Unless you are an insurance agent, it's quite confusing, isn't it? You feel that the information is very important for you but, try as you might, you just can't understand it. Finally, in bewilderment, you give up. If it's important enough at the time, you call your agent for help. So many people have felt confused when trying to read their policies that some companies now have illustrated contracts which use pictures to help the reader's understanding.

Confusion, then, is a natural feeling which has simple origins. When one has too many questions to answer or too many decisions to make thinking becomes somewhat disorganized. If one does not have the information needed to answer his questions the feeling of confusion is often heightened. It is to be expected that confusion would be an early reaction of parents when they learn that something is wrong with their child.

Most states of confusion are short-lived. The confused driver soon finds his street and number. Only in jokes does a driver spend a day trying to find his way off the freeway's clover leaf. The person with so much to do that he "doesn't know where to start" does start one job, finish it, go on to the next, and so on. As the work progresses the feeling of confusion lessens. For most persons, confusion is temporary and superficial. When the cause is removed the feeling disappears.

We often see parents of handicapped children with feelings of confusion of long duration. They began when the parents learned that something was wrong and continued for months and even years. Chronic confusion interferes with one's effectiveness. As has been pointed out, an important feature of confusion is disorganized thinking. Disorganized thinking leads to a lack of direction in one's activities. Some parents who haven't yet learned to recognize their feeling of confusion or learned how to deal with this feeling seem to be caught on dead center. They find it difficult to do anything. Others seem to be running off in many directions at the same time. They hardly start one thing before they give it up to start something else and they are often working ineffectively at many things simultaneously. Obviously, their behavior not only affects their own personal lives but also the lives of their families.

Anxiety Is an Offspring of Confusion

Unrecognized and unmanaged feelings of confusion can lead to deeper feelings of insecurity and anxiety. At their origin, insecurity and anxiety are not complicated feelings. To feel insecure is merely to be unsure about things. As any parent of a handicapped child knows, there are many things about which one is uncertain when he learns that something is wrong with his child. Too many uncertainties—too many things about which one feels unsure—give rise to feelings of insecurity. When a person has many questions milling around in his head he is confused. When he tries to answer the questions but is unsure of his answers and of himself he feels insecure. An insecure person often finds himself lacking in the self-confidence necessary for carrying out effectively the tasks of everyday living. Feelings of confusion and insecurity don't remain compartmentalized. When parents have unresolved feelings of confusion about their handicapped child's problems, their feelings about some other matters may become confused, also. This is because confusion tends to be an upsetting state of mind which affects our behavior widely rather than merely affecting a limited aspect of our thinking. It is generally recognized that people can do some strange things when they are feeling confused. Feelings of insecurity tend to spread, also. At first a parent feels insecure about the welfare of his child. When this feeling is not understood and properly managed, he finds himself feeling insecure about many things. As confusion and insecurity spread, a generalized uneasiness of mind develops. This is what is often called anxiety—the uneasiness of mind with the restlessness or nervousness which accompanies it.

In our clinics we often see parents who feel insecure and anxious. With most of these parents we can trace the development of these feelings back to the confusions which began when they learned something was wrong with their child.

In one of our group discussions a troubled mother said, "Yes, I admit I'm confused—hopelessly confused! What I want to know is what can I do about it?"

The mother of a retarded child spoke up, "Well, I found out that talking isn't enough. I just talked around in circles. I talked about my problems so much to everyone that soon my friends didn't want to see me anymore. Finally my sister said, 'Mary, you just keep saying the same things over and over until everyone's tired of listening to you. Why don't you try to learn more about Bobby's problem—get some new information.' This made me mad at first but when I thought about it more I realized she was right."

After a brief pause another mother added, "I know we all felt better when we learned something about cerebral palsy. The clinic gave us a booklet to read which told about the causes of cerebral palsy and what kinds of treatment are given to children who have cerebral palsy. My husband and I read it but it still took us awhile to get our thoughts organized. We had to find out what we should do, decide what we'd tell people, and all kinds of things."

There followed a discussion of getting information by reading books, asking questions of doctors and of other parents, etc. Finally a mother pointed out, "Too much information can be just as confusing as not enough. You have to watch what kind of books you read, too. I got a medical book from the library once and I couldn't make head or tail of it. These books don't help much unless they're written so you can understand them."

Another mother of a cerebral palsied child interrupted, "I agree with you that too much information can be confusing. When Joe was a baby I kept pestering the clinic to tell me whether he'd go to school and whether he'd be able to get a job and stuff like that. One day a therapist sat down with me and described in detail everything we were going to work at during the next six years. I threw up my hands and said, 'Not so fast, not so fast. Let's not try to do everything all at once.' When Joe and I were going home I got to thinging that maybe I had been asking questions that couldn't be answered yet."

This started a discussion about how much information parents needed and when should they get it. Most of the group felt that parents need general information about the nature of their child's problem; what might have caused it and what can be done about it. Many parents said they found it very helpful to learn how many other children had similar difficulties. All the parents agreed that even though they often asked for long-range predictions about progress, deep down inside they knew it was better to wait for awhile to see how the child was coming along.

When this discussion lagged, another mother who had been quiet during most of the session said, "I've been thinking about how we overcame our confusion and I think you've missed a very important point. I agree that you need information and you have to organize your thinking but, most of all, you have to do something. Carrying out the doctor's instructions for treatment, helping with a fund drive, or working with a parents' council will give you something positive to think about."

Confusion's Ill Effects May Be Prevented

In a one-hour period of guided discussion this small group of parents had identified three important antidotes to confusion:

1. Appropriate and accurate information obtained when needed and when the parents are ready for it.

Too much information given too soon can be as confusing as having too little information or getting your information too late. Inaccurate information can never be helpful. The best sources are the professional workers taking care of your child and booklets especially prepared for parents. Talking things over with other parents, especially those who have older children, can be very helpful.

2. Organization of thoughts and feelings.

To counteract confusion, information must be organized around key questions such as: "What is wrong with our child? What can be done about it? What should we, as parents, be doing?" Family thoughts and feelings seem to clear up faster when the father and mother work together at answering these questions. When the father and mother can go together to see the specialist, when they read the same booklets, etc., they can be of tremendous help to each other in thinking through the many questions which, when unanswered, are so upsetting.

3. Participation in a positive action program.

Having organized information will usually not be enough to dispel confused thoughts and feelings. Many parents find much personal satisfaction in a two-level action program. The first level, of course, consists of providing for their child all the examinations, treatment, special education, and other services recommended by the staff taking care of him. Acting only at this level, however, can lead to a narrow view of the child's difficulty. Perspective is gained by action on a second level which consists of working to improve the welfare of all handicapped children. Occasionally parents try to escape facing their responsibilities to their own children by concentrating all their efforts at level two—sometimes to the extent of becoming misguided zealots. Not only do they remain confused but they often succeed in confusing any issues with which they become identified. Occasionally an emotional approach is needed but continuing emotional appeals lose their effectiveness. Over the long term, the welfare of handicapped persons can best be served through a balanced, thoughtful support of projects organized in their interest. Parents of handicapped children probably always have some element of emotion behind their support of a "cause" but those whose motivations are predominantly rational rather than emotional are likely to be most effective. They are likely to be less confused, too!

I would add a fourth antidote for confusion to the three suggested by the parents in their group discussion. This would be *time.* Of course, time by itself will not eliminate confusion but it takes time to get information, to organize one's thoughts, and to become effectively participant in a positive action program. Parents should not expect, therefore, to overcome their feelings of confusion overnight.

Our discussion so far has been concerned with the feelings which develop when some professional person first discovers the child's handicap and reports it to the parents. Sometimes the parents themselves observe that the infant is not doing as well in sitting up, walking, talking, or other activities. They begin to suspect that something is wrong. When their suspicions are confirmed by the report of a specialist many of these parents also go through a period of confusion. They do not, however, experience the same feeling of shock which was reported by other parents on first learning that something is wrong. Instead, parents who gradually come to realize that something is wrong suffer what one parent called a period of "gnawing doubt and fear." She said she was actually relieved when the doctor told her that her child had cerebral palsy with a paralysis on the right side for she had been afraid it would be worse. This same point of view has often been echoed by other parents.

Parents Differ in Strength of Feeling

The strength of parental reactions seems to vary with the severity of the child's handicap. Generally speaking, the more severe the handicap, the stronger the parents' feelings. This is especially true when only limited habilitation may be expected as with mentally retarded or cerebral palsied children. Sometimes, however, parents whose children are only minimally handicapped become deeply agitated when told that their child is different from most children of the same age.

This reaction was seen in young parents whom I saw at the request of their pediatrician. They had recently been told by the school psychologist that their second-grade daughter was a slow learner and would get most out of school if she were in a class with other slow-learning children. The school personnel proposed transferring her immediately to such a group. The parents balked, pointing out that their daughter's marks in first grade had been satisfactory and they refused to accept the school's explanation that the previous marks had been based on effort rather than achievement. The parents insisted that the school marks were a better indication of their daughter's ability than the psychologist's evaluation. When the school psychologist offered to re-examine the child the parents objected saying they preferred to have her examined by an "outside" agency. The low marks Alice took home at the next grading period were interpreted as an attempt by the teacher and psychologist to "get even" with them. During the early part of our conference the father's face was flushed with anger as he talked about the school and his wife sat rigidly, bristling with hostility. My examination of Alice confirmed the school's findings that she was a slow learner—not markedly retarded but enough below average that she would encounter increasing difficulty in school unless she received special help. Her memory was as good as that of other second grade children but her reasoning ability was quite poor. She could read fluently from a second-grade book but didn't understand much of what she read. She could count but had not grasped the idea of adding and subtracting. As the parents and I discussed my findings the father volunteered that Alice was much slower than her sisters. A businessman, he had tried to teach her about money. She had learned the names of various coins but "couldn't even learn that two nickels make a dime." He said, "She's pretty slow when it comes to getting jokes and teasing." Then came a torrent of questions: "What would Alice's playmates think if she changed to another class? Why hadn't the school told them about this sooner? Would Alice be able to have a boy friend of her age when she reached seventeen or eighteen? What did they do in this special class, anyhow?"

As we talked, he calmed down and his wife began to relax. He now conceded that the school was on the right track in wanting to put Alice with a slower group but insisted that the school authorities had certainly not handled this problem properly. With this point of view one must agree because here again we see the professionals concentrating on the child's problem and providing little help for the parents. The agitation of these parents had grown completely out of proportion to the size of the problem which set it off. It would have continued to grow had not the parents had an opportunity to talk through their feelings with someone who was interested in them as well as in their child.

An Unfavorable Diagnosis Is Hard to Accept

It is not always possible for even a sensitive and highly skilled counselor to prevent parents from becoming upset upon learning that something is wrong with their child. To learn that one's child has some life-long handicap such as cerebral palsy or mental retardation is, of course, much more disconcerting than to learn that he has some temporary ailment such as measles. It would be an insensitive parent, indeed, who would not feel concerned when told that his child has a handicapping disability. In our culture, every parent nurses the hope that his child will climb to a higher rung on the ladder of success than the parents have reached. A natural defense against the dashing of this hope is to doubt the diagnosis and seek more favorable opinions from other doctors or clinics. Some parents become "shoppers," taking their child here and there hoping someone will say nothing is wrong and that everything will eventually be all right. Their ears are tuned to hear only what they want to be told and they often reject any counsel based on a realistic evaluation of their child's condition. In addition to the parents' concern, two factors operate to perpetuate these "shopping tours": the attitude and approach of professional workers often fail to engender confidence in the parents and, hence, naturally give rise to doubts; there is not developed the continuing relationship between family and professional worker which leads to mutual understanding.

When parents of handicapped children meet in small groups for counseling, it may be predicted that an early topic of discussion will be their feelings toward the professional workers with whom they first discussed their child's problem. To hear many parents talk one would be led to conclude that practically all doctors are incompetent and without feeling. At one session of group counseling the parents had been particularly critical of the doctors who had cared for their children. One after another they released long pent-up feelings. The mother of a cerebral palsied child said, speaking of her doctor, "He kept telling me that nothing was wrong and that I was just a tense mother. Finally, when our baby didn't start walking, he had to admit I had been right all along and that something was wrong. He said he had known it but didn't want to worry me. I'll never forgive him for that!"

Another mother said, "Well, that's a lot better than my doctor did. He took one look at Carol Ann and told us to put her in an institution. I cried for days. Can you imagine anything so heartless?"

"What makes us so mad is that the doctor never really spends any time with us," said the mother of a multiply handicapped child. "It's just as if he knows he can't do anything and he doesn't want to be bothered. The first time he saw Jimmy he said he had a lot of things wrong with him and he never tells us any more than that. We've decided to start hunting until we find a doctor we like."

There was much talking in this vein with each mother anxious to cite examples of how she was mistreated by her doctors. When the comments began to come more slowly I asked, "Have you ever heard of a parent who felt good about the way he learned something was wrong with his child?"

Somewhat hostilely a mother began, "How could a parent feel good? The doctors are all so busy . . ."

"Or we're all so unhappy," another mother interrupted. "Maybe most of the trouble is in us and not the doctors. I'll bet some of us would even hate the Almighty if He'd be the one to tell us the bad news."

Continuity of Treatment Is Essential

It's quite natural for parents to have ill feelings toward the doctor or other professional worker who told them that something was wrong with the child. By failing to consider parents' problems along with those of the child, the behavior of professional workers sometimes provides nourishment for these ill feelings. It is unfortunate for the parents and the handicapped child when parents are driven by their attitudes to shop around for a more favorable diagnosis or a doctor or clinic they like better. Continuity of care and treatment is essential if a child is to achieve his maximal level of habilitation. Continuity is not possible when a child is shifted from one program to another. This is not to say that a professional worker is always one hundred percent accurate in his diagnosis or evaluation. Sometimes it is necessary to study a child over a period of time to establish an evaluation and to plan an appropriate treatment program. Before changing doctors or running off to another clinic, parents should ask themselves, "Do I really think these professional people don't know what's wrong with my child and what to do about it, or am I mad at them because they gave me bad news?" When a genuine doubt about the diagnosis exists in the parent's mind it is always advisable for parents to explain these doubts and say that they would like to get another opinion. Rarely will a doctor or clinic refuse to refer a family to another facility for a consultation. This procedure makes for a better coordination of efforts and for better program continuity. It also prevents the confusion which arises from "shopping."

———

Wouldn't it be most unusual for parents to feel good upon learning that something was wrong with their child? Surely we would feel that something was wrong with them as parents. The kinds of reactions parents have when they learn something is wrong are natural and to be expected. When they are recognized, understood, and properly directed these reactions cause no serious problems. Only when they are allowed to grow unchecked do they develop into troublesome feelings and attitudes. Parents usually have within themselves the ability to check the development of the troubled feelings which begin when they learn that something is wrong with their child.

III

Unfulfilled Expectations

Have you ever wanted something very much and looked forward eagerly to getting it only to find when you finally got it that it wasn't what you had expected? How did you feel?

One time when a group of parents was discussing feelings of disappointment a young mother told us how she had "saved and saved" to get a new dress. She had in mind one that had looked "simply gorgeous" on a model in a store window and, to her delight, the store had one in her size. All the way home she kept thinking of the dress in the box tucked under her arm and the accessories she would wear with it to a party her husband's boss was giving. She couldn't wait to try it on for her husband who had been hearing about this dress for days. Her heart fell when he said, "Honey, it's a pretty dress but is it your style?" The mirror confirmed the appropriateness of his question. She said, "I felt terribly let down and disappointed because I had wanted that dress so much."

Another mother told how she had planned to serve a special cake to her bridge club because the girls always tried to outdo each other at making desserts. She had carefully followed the recipe and while the cake was baking she got dressed for the party. When the timer rang she opened the oven only to find a "sunken, brown mess instead of the fluffy, light cake I had expected." She said, "I was so disappointed I just sat down and cried."

When I give a talk to a group about the feelings of parents of handicapped children, I often ask the audience, "How many of you have ever been disappointed in your life?" Almost everyone raises his hand. Sometimes I ask members of the audience to tell about some situation in which they were disappointed. The details of the experiences differ but the underlying cause of the feeling of disappointment is always the same. Disappointment is a natural reaction to unfulfilled expectations. A coed might tell of her excitement at being invited to the prom by a popular senior and the depression which swept over her when the date was cancelled because he caught the flu and was confined to the infirmary on the eve of the dance. A father might tell of a hunting trip he had planned with three other fellows and his dejected feelings when they went off without him because he had to work. A woman might tell of making arrangements to travel across the country to see her mother and sister whom she hadn't seen for years and being forced to cancel her plans at the last minute because her husband became ill. Whatever the details of the experience there is in disappointment always the element of anticipation or expectation followed by failure of that which was expected to come about. The poet, Alexander Pope, recognized the origin of disappointment and suggested as a ninth beatitude: "Blessed is he who expects nothing, for he shall never be disappointed."

Just as people are disappointed when a dress or a cake doesn't turn out as expected or a trip doesn't work out as planned, parents can become disappointed when a child is found to be not as normal as his parents wanted him to be. Most children, even those who aren't "planned," are wanted children and their parents usually have great expectations for them. They expect that their child will walk like other children, talk like other children, go to school, get a job, get married, and do all the things other people do. When it becomes apparent that because of some handicapping condition of the child these expectations can at best be only partially realized, disappointment naturally sets in.

Disappointment Affects Parent-Child Relationship

Most disappointment is superficial and temporary but the disappointment associated with having a handicapped child often is deep and long lasting. It can adversely influence the parents' relationships with the handicapped child by creating psychological barriers between parent and child. Parents whose feelings of disappointment are strong sometimes find it difficult to give their handicapped child the warm affection and acceptance which are important for his emotional growth. This was the problem of the father of a 9-year-old cerebral palsied boy who was severely involved in all four limbs. John's father, a big handsome lawyer, had been a varsity football player in college and, as he told me, he had looked forward to the day when he could sit in the grandstand and watch his boy play. "Look," he said, "he's nine years old and can't even walk. How can he ever play football? How can he ever play anything?" As we talked he told how he felt "unhappy" and "let down" everytime he tried to play with his boy. "Now," he said, "it's got so I just can't bring myself to play with him any more. I keep thinking, what's the use? He's never going to be able to do anything." John's father had expected a big, strong son who would follow in his footsteps. His expectations weren't realized and his disappointment went deep. When, through counseling, he learned to recognize his feelings of disappointment and to see how these feelings were related to his expectations he began to feel and act differently toward John. Although he continued to feel some disappointment that his son would never be an athlete, he was able to control his feelings. Realizing that he couldn't play ball with his son as he expected, he began teaching him about sports and athletes. He learned to find companionship with his son in watching games together. Through learning to recognize and understand his feelings of disappointment and learning how to do things with his son he was able to lessen the bitterness of his disappointment.

A mother's expectations, too, can lead to deep disappointment when her child is handicapped. Jane's mother was an attractive and talented woman. She played the piano and sang well, but the hobby of which she was most proud was her sewing. She made most of her own clothing—dresses, suits, coats, etc. People were always complimenting her on how nice she looked and were quite impressed upon learning that she had made her own clothes. Tearfully she told me, "I had always looked forward to having a daughter so I could dress her in pretty clothes. I'd planned to make her all kinds of dresses and skirts and coats—but, look at Janie. With those ugly braces she can't look good in anything!"

Robert Burns described the plight of Janie's mother, John's father, and all of us who plan with high hopes:

> *The best laid schemes of mice and men*
> *Gang aft a-gley;*
> *And leave us nought but grief and pain,*
> *For promised joy.*

Disappointment is a very natural feeling when plans go astray. An occasional disappointment is usually of small moment in our lives. When one suffers repeated disappointments, however, or when one has a deep disappointment of which he cannot rid himself, he may develop unwholesome reactions toward the source of the disappointment. In this natural reaction we can find the genesis of much of the rejection which sometimes separates a parent and a handicapped child.

Disappointment May Be General

Not always is the disappointment directly related to some specific expectation as it was in the case of John's father and Jane's mother. Probably more often parents experience a general kind of disappointment. The mother of a mentally retarded child once told me that every time she thought about her child she felt disappointed that he wasn't normal. She said, "I just can't get it out of my mind that he won't be able to live a normal life. I know there isn't much anyone can do to help him so I just feel frustrated and disappointed." The mother of a deaf child said, "Everytime I hear music or a bird or our cat purring I feel sad because I know Tim will never hear these sounds. And when I think about how poor his speech is I can't understand why this had to happen. I'd like to know why we couldn't have a boy who could hear and talk like other children! Do other parents feel like I do?"

Troubled Feelings Originate in Disappointment

The answer, of course, is Yes. Most parents feel disappointed when they learn their child will not be like other children. In fact, disappointment is such a natural reaction to unfulfilled expectations that a parent of a handicapped child could hardly avoid feeling disappointed. When its origins are recognized and the nature of its feelings understood, disappointment is not a serious or unwholesome feeling. Disappointment becomes a problem only when it grows into feelings of sorrow and grief or stands in the way of a parent's accepting a child. When parents encounter an emotional block to their acceptance of their child, the stage is set for a chain of undesirable reactions to occur. It is common and natural for parents who emotionally reject their child to become oversolicitous toward him. They shower a superficial kind of attention on him, become over-protective and in other ways try to hide, even from themselves, their true feelings toward the child. Over-solicitousness and over-protectiveness interfere with the social and physical development of the handicapped child because they prevent him from having the kinds of experience which are basic to learning and to the development of independence. When parents, for any reason, devote all their time and resources to the handicapped child, other children in the family sometimes feel neglected. More than once we have heard of normal children who wished that they were crippled so that they could get some of the attention which their parents seem to reserve for the handicapped child. Neglect of normal siblings is more likely to occur when parents try to compensate for their rejection of a handicapped child. Despite all parents can do to "cover up," handicapped children are quick to sense their parents' disappointment. Their awareness of being rejected by their parents depresses their feelings of personal worth. They begin to develop the inferiority feelings which lower their level of aspiration and weaken their drive to achieve. From simple disappointment, complex psychological reactions may develop. It is much easier to learn to manage one's feelings of disappointment than to untwist the chain of reactions which may develop from them.

Parents Can Manage Disappointments

When parent groups have discussed how one gets over feelings of disappointment, several helpful suggestions have been made:

A mother expressed the feelings of many parents when she said, "Just learning that disappointment was a natural reaction when things didn't turn out as you hoped helped soften my feelings."

A father said, "When I saw how my disappointment was related to my expectations I decided I'd better change my expectations. After all, why should we decide what a child's going to be like even before he's born? Maybe if my boy'd been normal he wouldn't want to do the things I want to do. You won't be so disappointed if you think of your kid instead of yourself."

Another told one of our groups, "At first all I could think of was all the things Joe couldn't do and I was disappointed all the time. My husband started pointing out some things Joe could do and soon I began to look for things to tell my husband. When I began thinking about what he could do I didn't feel so disappointed."

"Doing something helps, too," another parent suggested. "Moping around and feeling sorry for yourself isn't any good. If you're doing all that needs to be done for your own child and doing something to help other handicapped children your mind won't have much room for disappointment."

Here, as stated by parents of handicapped children, are four effective suggestions for counteracting the feelings of disappointment which naturally appear when one has a handicapped child. They may be restated as follows:

1. Learn that disappointment is a natural reaction to unfulfilled expectations.

Disappointment may be superficial or deep, temporary or long lasting. Most disappointment is superficial and of short duration. The disappointment associated with having a handicapped child usually is deep and long lasting. Disappointment is not an emotionally unhealthy problem unless it develops into frustration or grief or interferes with the parents' emotional acceptance of the handicapped child.

2. Change expectations.

Since disappointment results from failure to realize an expectation, the degree of disappointment is often related to the nature of the expectation. Often expectations are developed in terms of parental interests or ambitions rather than in terms of children's capacities. The stage is set for developing bitter disappointment when parents set unrealistic goals for their children. As long as the gap between the child's potential and the parents' expectations remains great, parental disappointment is bound to occur. When the child's potential cannot be raised, only by modifying his expectations can the parent reduce his disappointment.

3.   Think of the child's capabilities as well as his liabilities.

Refusing to recognize a handicapped child's limitations will lead to the development of an unobjective and unrealistic attitude. Concentration on his limitations while ignoring his capabilities will contribute to parental disappointment. Parents can be most helpful to their children and to themselves by making an accurate appraisal of their child's capabilities and his limitations. "Accentuating the positive and eliminating the negative," as advised by a songwriter, is not a sure road to overcoming the disappointment of having a handicapped child. The "negative" is there and must be recognized if effective planning is to be done for the child. Some "positive" elements are also present and they, too, must be considered. Finding them helps relieve the feeling of parental disappointment.

4.   Become involved in a positive action program.

Doing something constructive is always an effective antidote to undesirable feelings such as confusion and disappointment. In our discussion of ways to overcome confusion suggestions were made about participation in a positive action program. They are equally pertinent here.

Following one discussion of disappointment in which many suggestions for overcoming this feeling were offered, one parent made the others all stop and think by her question—"Do parents of handicapped children ever completely get over their disappointment?" No one said anything for quite a long time then an older mother said, "No, I don't think so. You can do some things to weaken it and time wears it down some but a little of it always stays in the back of your mind. It comes out when you are lying awake in the middle of the night or when you see that your child can't do something that he wants to do."

After another pause, someone else said, "I guess that's right. We should do what we can to understand and lessen our disappointment, but we'd better not expect to get rid of all of it. After all, we did say that disappointment is a normal reaction, didn't we?"

IV

What Will People Think?

It is probably safe to say that no one is completely unconcerned about what other people think. Even the person who
considers himself to be a rugged individualist often wants to
be sure that others are aware of his independence of thought
and action. A few persons seem to delight in saying or doing
things which shock others but the aim of most of us is to engender a favorable reaction to our words and behavior. Our
need to be accepted by others is an important motivating force
in our lives. So strong is this force that thoughtful Americans
fear that our need to be accepted is making conformists of us
all. Just how dangerous this trend might be need not concern
us here but that there is such a trend is obvious. Unfortunately, not only do we select our clothing to be "in style" but more

and more we find our thinking and actions following the currently accepted pattern. Most of us carefully refrain from word or deed which will mark us as being different. We avoid controversy. We are anxious to do nothing which will lower our standing or lessen our acceptance by the persons with whom we associate. From infancy on man is eager to be accepted.

I recall talking with a professional man of Oriental ancestry who felt apart from everyone in the community. He felt sure that because of his appearance everyone felt that he was of an inferior race. He was unhappy in his loneliness and his moods alternated between being angry with everyone and being doubtful of his personal worth. Because he was not like the other people with whom he might associate he felt that he was not acceptable to them. When I asked some of his associates why he seemed to have difficulty making friends they said it was because he was so timid and had so much trouble talking with people. Not one of them mentioned his appearance or race as a factor unless I asked about it. Their comments then suggested that his attitude rather than his appearance or race prevented his making friends and developing a social life. He was so much concerned about what people were thinking of him that he couldn't feel comfortable in a group and he often, without reason, assumed that people didn't like him. Of course, we know, as he knew, that there are people who find it difficult to accept another person of a different race, creed, color, social status, or who in some other way fails to meet the established standard of the group. Often, though, other people are much more accepting and much less aware of differences than the "different" individual realizes.

This need for acceptance by their associates is very strong among teen-agers and results in a uniform pattern of dress, speech, and behavior which is often distressing to their elders. When blue jeans and sneakers are the rage a parental suggestion that a skirt and shoes would be more appropriate brings the lament, "Do you want the other kids to think I'm crazy or something?"

Attitudes and Behavior Affect Acceptance

The preparations made by a bride for the first visit of her husband's parents show how eager she is to win their approval—to be accepted by them. The house must be in order with not a speck of dust anywhere and the menu must demonstrate that their son is being well fed. She feels that she is under observation all during the visit and worries that her house, her meals, in fact, she herself might not pass the critical inspection of her mother-in-law. Few brides and grooms assume that acceptance by their in-laws comes automatically at the conclusion of the marriage ceremony. Most of them feel a need to make a good impression on uncles, aunts, and cousins as well as on their mate's immediate family. Acceptance as a member of the family, they realize, must be earned so they are careful to be on their good behavior when relatives are around.

This same need for acceptance was seen in the reaction of a young mother when she learned that her child was mentally retarded. Noting her worried look, I asked, "What are you mostly concerned about?"

"How can I tell my relatives and what will they think," she replied.

"Are you wondering if you can make them understand why Bobby doesn't learn as quickly as other children?" I asked her

"Oh, they'll understand that all right," was her quick retort. Then, after a pause, "They'll never forgive me for bringing a child like this into the family."

Just like the bride who felt that producing an inferior meal for her relatives would lessen their acceptance of her, this mother felt that producing an inferior child would earn her the disapproval of her relatives. She needed to be accepted by them and very naturally was worried that their approval, which she had tried to earn, might now be withdrawn.

The mother of a newborn baby with a cleft lip and cleft palate told her doctor that she did not want to take her baby home from the hospital until its lip was repaired. The doctor, suspecting that she was afraid she could not take care of the infant because of the cleft, explained that she would not have any problems in feeding the baby.

"It isn't that," she said. "I just don't want our relatives and friends to see him like this!"

The doctor explained that usually no surgery was done until the baby had regained his birthweight and was getting along well.

"What will they think of us with his face all open like that?" she commented. "Even after the operation they'll always remember how he looked when he was born."

Here again we see a natural concern: "What will people think?" This mother was outspoken in her concern. Many others are just as concerned about what people will think but inhibit expression of their feelings. Often their concern grows greater because it remains unspoken.

The father of a cerebral palsied boy gave the need for acceptance a somewhat different emphasis when he asked, "Where do handicapped people find friends? I think you have to do things with people to establish friendships. If a kid can't do anything how can he get people to like him?" This father was aware of our natural desires to be liked—to be accepted—and was concerned that his boy would be handicapped in gaining affection, approval, and other evidences of acceptance.

Parents Resent Persons Who Withhold Acceptance

Many times I have listened to parents tell of how their feelings were hurt when their handicapped child did not fit into a birthday party or some other entertainment. Some parents have told of becoming "fighting mad" when other children have refused to include their handicapped child in play activities or when a visit to a friend's home left them feeling unwelcome. These feelings are easy to understand. Acceptance is needed by each of us. When it is withheld or withdrawn we are hurt and perhaps become angry. It is in human nature for us to feel like fighting if our children are not accepted as we think they should be.

In a series of discussion sessions parents usually get around to talking about how their relatives and friends, in fact, the public in general, do not accept them or their handicapped child. As a rule, there is some airing of feelings with each parent emotionally describing some incidences of nonacceptance. At this point the tone of the discussion is quite negative with the "other" person always depicted in an unfavorable light. After the parents have let off steam their discussion may be turned into more positive directions by asking, "Are there any things parents can do when they feel they are not being accepted?" In one group, when this question followed an airing period, a father responded, "I think we need to understand our need to be accepted. It sounds to me as if some of us push ourselves and our children into situations where we shouldn't expect people to accept us. Maybe we want to be accepted so much that we push too hard for it."

Another parent added, "I think that's right and we need to recognize, too, that some people just find it difficult to accept anyone who is different. You see this all the time in prejudice against Negroes, or Jews, or Catholics. Staunch Republicans can't stand Democrats and vice versa. I guess we just got to expect that there will always be some people who won't find it easy to like handicapped children and maybe even their parents."

A third parent interrupted, "I agree with both of you but I'm sure that most people are probably more accepting than we give them credit for. As I listened to all our talk about the people who wouldn't accept us I couldn't help feeling that sometimes we just take things the wrong way. Lots of us carry chips on our shoulders. We just think that people aren't going to accept us so we misinterpret everything they say or do to prove our point."

This group had recognized three very important points. We all know people who are so hungry for approval and acceptance that they almost ask outright for it. Their eagerness to be liked actually discourages people from liking them. They try so hard to achieve status that they get into their own way and the status they strive for is denied them. The mother of a 10-year-old cerebral palsied girl once told me, "We take Sarah every place we go—to church, to restaurants, to visit our friends. We never go anyplace without her." Knowing that

Sarah couldn't walk or talk and couldn't feed herself, I wondered how wise they were. It would seem that socially mature parents should be going some places where it would not be appropriate to take a 10-year-old girl even if she were not severely handicapped. Thoughtful parents have recognized an obligation to consider the feelings of others. They have tempered their desire to provide social experiences for their handicapped children with an awareness that there are some times and occasions when parents should go alone leaving their child in good care. When thoughtful parents feel that they or their children are not being accepted they ask themselves, "Am I really not being accepted or is this just my imagination?" Sometimes it is just imagination. In those situations when some relatives or friends are not able to accept the handicapped child, parents need to think through what they can do to change this attitude. Merely forcing oneself into the situation rarely results in gaining acceptance and withdrawing is usually just as ineffective.

A mother once told me that when it was discovered that her son was cerebral palsied and mentally retarded, "Everyone let me down. All of our relatives and even my husband acted as if it was all my fault. I got so I didn't want to go anyplace anymore or talk to anyone."

When I asked her if she had ever discussed her boy's condition with her relatives or friends she replied, "Oh, no! I couldn't do that. They just wouldn't understand. If anyone ever asks anything about him I steer the conversation to another topic."

When I was talking with her husband he commented with bitter resignation, "No, Agnes won't talk about the boy's problem. I think she wants to bear her cross alone and if that's the way she wants it, I guess that's the way it'll have to be."

There are a few parents who react to having a handicapped child by casting themselves in the role of martyrs. Their martyrdom requires that they cut themselves off from other people but, not understanding their own feelings, they accuse others of letting them down, of not accepting them or their child. But Agnes' husband was wrong for she was no martyr. She wanted and needed someone to talk to. When I asked her to tell me what she understood was wrong with her son, what had caused it, and what could be done about it, I found she couldn't. In the first place she actually knew very little about his difficulty and secondly talking about it made her so emotionally upset that she couldn't talk coherently about what she did know. To protect herself she just "steered the conversation to another topic." Like her husband, her friends and relatives misunderstood her and became quite uncomfortable when with her.

Many parents have reported that friends and relatives have become more understanding and accepting following a frank, objective discussion of a handicapped child's condition. This point was made by the parents of a young deaf girl. The mother said, "At first we didn't talk about Linda's problem with our family or anyone else. This topic was strictly taboo. We figured it was a personal thing and no one else's business."

Her husband interjected, "We wanted people to think of her just like they thought about other children. We figured if we told them too much about her condition they would think only about her problem and not think about her as a little girl."

"What happened to make you change your approach?" I asked.

"Well," answered the mother, "we began to notice that some

of our friends seemed to be a little cool toward us and were ill at ease when Linda was around."

"Then one day my wife overheard some of the neighbors talking about Linda," said the father. "They were discussing why she didn't talk. One of them said she might be feeble-minded. Another thought she might have trouble with her tongue or her lungs. Another lady said, 'I think she doesn't hear right but if that's it I can't understand why her parents don't tell us about it.' "

"And then the one who thought Linda might be feeble-minded said, 'Maybe they're ashamed of what caused it,' and that made me boil," the mother added. "I almost walked over and gave them a piece of my mind right then and there."

These parents went on to tell that they suddenly realized that you couldn't keep people from wondering and talking. Their own reticence had backfired. Not only were their associates talking about Linda's problem but they were speculating about why the parents were so secretive. They decided it was better to be honest and open in talking about Linda's problem instead of being evasive and secretive.

Sometimes the feelings of other people are reflections of our own feelings. Thackery, in *Vanity Fair,* wrote:

> *The world is a looking glass, and gives back*
> *to every man the reflection of his own face. Frown*
> *at it, and it will in turn look sourly upon you;*
> *laugh at it and with it, and it is a jolly, kind*
> *companion.*

More than one parent has come to realize that at the same

time he is distressed because other people don't accept his child, he is also finding it difficult to give the warmth and affection which are synonymous with acceptance. The reactions of other people to his handicapped child may be a mirroring of his own reactions. The father described earlier who was disappointed because he could never sit in the grandstand and watch his boy play football said that as he got over his disappointment other people seemed to react more favorably to his boy. When asked how this could be, he replied, "Everyone seemed to sense how disappointed I was and they just held back on being nice or saying anything nice to Johnny. Maybe they figured I'd think they weren't sincere or maybe they thought they'd hurt my feelings. Anyhow, after I warmed up to him I noticed that a lot of other people warmed up to him, too."

The mother of a child born with a cleft lip told a group of mothers, "When I was all mixed up inside about the baby it just seemed that visitors didn't know what to say or how to act when they saw the baby. They'd stand around and act like they were afraid to say the wrong thing. When I got straightened up and could look at the baby without wanting to cry our families and neighbors were more at ease, too. You might say they were taking their cue from me. I'm sure that our own feelings about our handicapped children influence the feelings of other people!"

This observation was further amplified in the comments of the parents of a 10-year-old boy who was severely mentally retarded. They wanted to discuss with me the care of their child and were trying to decide if they should continue to keep him at home with them or arrange for him to enter a state residential program. During our discussion I asked how the neighbors reacted to Vernon.

"I don't know for sure," answered the mother. "On days when I'm feeling low and think we just can't go on this way much longer it seems that everyone around wants me to send him to a state home. On days when he's not much trouble and I'm feeling better about things the neighbors seem to be more understanding and friendly. Now, I don't know whether they change or I just see things in a different light as my mood changes."

"I'm sure it's both," said her husband. "When you feel bad yourself it seems that everyone is against you but there's plenty of reason for the neighbors to get mad, though, when Vernon runs around and gets into things. I've noticed that sometimes their reactions depend on how disturbed we are but I'm sure we couldn't change all their feelings about Vernon simply by changing our own. Maybe we've got to try harder to manage Vernon better, too."

Vernon's father had hit on another important thing parents can do when they feel they or their handicapped child are not being accepted, that is, change the child's appearance or behavior so as to make him more acceptable. This point was made very honestly by the father of a 6-year-old boy who was so severely handicapped by cerebral palsy that he couldn't feed himself and was not yet bladder and bowel trained. His wife was complaining that everyone seemed to draw away from their son and no one invited them anyplace or even dropped in for a visit.

"Let's be honest about it, honey," her husband said. "Johnnie often isn't pleasant to be around."

His wife looked shocked by his comment and started to reply but he interrupted, "You know how hard it is to feed him. He gets food all over his face and his clothes and his shirt gets wet from drooling. We're used to it now but he's often unsightly and sometimes he doesn't smell so good either. I think you have to expect neighbors and friends to be bothered by him. Maybe people will like him better when we can keep him cleaner."

The parents of a 9-year-old brain-damaged child were accusing their neighbors and friends of being intolerant toward their child. The mother said, "They are mean about it. They come right out and say they don't want Ray in their house. I know they allow other kids in to play but they're cruel and tell Ray to go home."

Her husband was angrily nodding his head in agreement, "and they don't want Ray to play with their kids outdoors, either. Our neighbor and I almost came to blows when I saw him send Ray home but let the other kids keep on playing ball in his yard."

We talked together several times and they came to see that Ray was hyperactive and had developed little self control. In part these characteristics were results of his brain damage but to some extent they were the results of misguided parental permissiveness. Aware that Ray had suffered some brain damage at birth, his parents explained all his behavior in terms of his organic problem. Believing discipline would be harmful to him, they laid down no rules and set no boundaries thus permitting him to do much as he wanted. His mother remarked that their home was usually a "wreck" and looked like "a cyclone had struck it." He ran, knocked things over, took things apart, and, as his father said, "was into everything."

"Nothing is ever safe when Ray's around!" agreed his mother.

When playing with other children Ray was unconcerned about the rules of a game. Actually, he didn't play with them. Rather, in his indifference to rules he interfered with their play. Sometimes his play was dangerous as when he would whirl a ball bat around his head or push children off the porch steps or thoughtlessly throw whatever he had in his hands. In telling about these things his father always said, "Of course, Ray never means any harm."

Gradually his parents came to recognize that other people did not accept Ray because his behavior was, in plain truth, unacceptable. Neighbors and friends were justified in feeling that they did not want their homes to look as if "a cyclone had struck" them. While it was true that Ray never meant any harm other parents knew, too, that involuntary manslaughter is unintentional. They had an obligation to protect their children from Ray's uncontrolled activity. Since his parents had failed to help Ray learn to control his behavior and made no effort to discipline him, the neighbors had to find a way of managing him. They did—through rejection, the opposite of acceptance. While some relaxation of the neighbors' attitudes might result from a discussion of Ray's problems, it does not seem reasonable to expect them to do all the adjusting. Ray's parents had an obligation to change their attitudes and to try to help him change his behavior. In other words, they might increase their acceptance by making themselves more acceptable.

It is evident that the need to be accepted can exert a strong influence on the feelings of parents of handicapped children. Thoughtful parents have suggested several things which might be done when parents feel that others are not accepting them or their child. These suggestions might be restated and amplified as follows:

1. *Understand the need for acceptance.*

The need to have the approval of others—to be accepted by them is a basic motivating force for everyone at all ages. Generally we try to say and do things which others will regard favorably. It is natural, therefore, for parents to ask—"What will people think?"—when a handicapped child is born. Parents seem to expect that others will react unfavorably to them and the handicapped child and that this unfavorable reaction will result in unfulfillment of their need for acceptance. While this need to be accepted is common to everyone, the granting of approval and acceptance in not automatic. Usually acceptance must be earned.

2. *Recognize that some people find it difficult to accept anyone who is different.*

It seems to be true that intolerance and prejudice are learned. No infant is born with anti-Semitic, anti-Catholic, or anti-Negro feelings. Such feelings are learned in very subtle ways without one's being aware that he is being taught. Once intolerance and prejudice become entwined in our thinking it is difficult to uproot them. Sometimes people want to be accepting of others but find themselves unable to react in a warm, friendly manner because of certain attitudes which block their offering of approval and acceptance. For similar reasons some people find it difficult to accept handicapped children and their parents. Forcing oneself on these people will seldom gain greater acceptance from them.

3. Become aware that most people are more accepting than you might expect.

Since parents expect unfavorable reactions to themselves and their handicapped children they often become oversensitive and misinterpret the words or actions of others. Most people feel an obligation to be helpful to handicapped persons and furthermore by nature they are understanding and sympathetic. Where people feel ill at ease with handicapped persons it is often because they do not know what to say or do rather than that they don't accept the handicapped person. By putting other people at ease, parents of handicapped children can often help create a climate of acceptance for themselves and their children. The climate of acceptance is usually present but remains obscured by a cloud of uncertainty in the minds of others as to how they should act or what they should say. Hesitance on the part of friends and relatives is often misinterpreted by parents as a lack of acceptance.

4. Be willing to discuss your child's problem honestly when occasion arises.

The inability to accept a handicapped child has an emotional rather than an intellectual basis. Misinformation or a lack of information often leads to a misunderstanding of the nature of a handicapped child's problem. In the absence of correct information imaginations run freely and many unfavorable opinions about the handicapped child and his family develop which take on undesirable emotional tones. Secretiveness on the part of the handicapped child's parents merely reinforces these adverse opinions and feelings. A parental willingness to supply correct information about the nature of a child's handicapping condition will help create a climate of acceptance among friends and relatives.

5. Learn that the feelings of others are often a reflection of your own feelings.

Both consciously and unconsciously people pattern their behavior to match that of other people. In a potentially embarrassing situation we sometimes deliberately watch the involved persons for cues as to how we should react. We often find ourselves feeling happy or sad because we have caught the mood of those around us without being aware of it. In a like manner friends and relatives may react to a handicapped child in the same way his parents react. Parental uncertainty, disappointment, non-acceptance, etc., beget similar feelings in others who are associated with the handicapped child.

6. Increase the handicapped child's acceptability.

Friends, neighbors, relatives—all people—have rights and sensitivities. When these are violated or ignored people naturally react unfavorably. Simple fairness demands that parents not repeatedly allow an unclean child to offend the sensitivities of others or an uncontrolled child to violate their rights. Most people are willing to make exceptions on occasion but practically everyone resents repeated offenses and violations, especially when the handicapped child's parents appear negligent or unconcerned.

Too Helpful People Create Problems

Surprising as it might seem, problems of handicapped persons sometimes arise because people are too accepting. An intelligent young woman who has been paralyzed in both legs since childhood says that many of her problems, both physical and psychological, are caused by people who want to be helpful. She has learned to get around quite satisfactorily with braces and crutches if permitted to move at her own pace. She drives her own car, lives alone in an apartment, and in every way is an independent person. She has no difficulty in making friends and enjoys giving small bridge and dinner parties. When allowed to function on her own with only the assistance she asks for, this young woman leads a life which is normal in most respects. It often happens, however, that well-intentioned people upset her balance by taking her arm to help her up or down steps, or over a curb or some other obstacle. Attempts to help her sit down or get up interfere with the pattern of her movements she has carefully developed. She says it is difficult to accept such "help" graciously, yet she knows a refusal or rebuff would offend or embarrass the one proffering assistance. For a long time she had difficulty managing these situations. If she turned down the help it sometimes made the person offering assistance feel foolish or ill-at-ease. If she accepted she often found herself in difficulty. Finally she found she could handle most offers to be of help to everyone's satisfaction by redirecting the helpfulness. When someone offers to take her arm on steps she says, "Thank you. I believe I can manage if you would just carry these books to the top of the stairs." Or, "Would you mind just walking behind me so no one will bump me." Just as a "helpful" person can physically knock her off balance, an overly solicitous person can upset her psychologically. Associates who are not aware of the fullness of her social and personal life sometimes try to plan for her. Not content with extending a social invitation to her as they might to everyone else, they try to interest her in various clubs, arrange opportunities for her to meet people, almost push her into various social situations, and, as she says, never give her a moment's peace. Here, again, she has had to learn how to let these people know that she is socially independent without rebuffing them.

This problem of over-acceptance is not peculiar to the adult handicapped. One evening, before a discussion session with a group of parents, I overheard the following discussion between two mothers who had arrived early:

"What do you do about people who think because you have a handicapped child you can't do anything for yourself?" asked the first mother. Then she added, "They make me so mad!"

"I know what you mean," said the second mother. "It's just like they're throwing in your face all the time that something's wrong and they have to help you out."

"No, not exactly that," replied the first mother. "It's more that they get in the way and aren't helpful at all. They interfere and I could get along better by myself."

"That's true, too, but sometimes they make me mad because they're always making me aware that we have a crippled child," said the second mother. "One of our neighbors is always sending us pie and cake because she says she knows I don't have time to bake. I guess her heart's in the right place but I think she overdoes it. My husband calls all her cakes 'Johnny cake' because Johnny's the name of our crippled boy."

Some other parents arrived and the conversation ended with the relating of this poignant pun. The talk turned to other matters and this topic did not come up again in the discussion session. The initial question—"What do you do about people who think because you have a handicapped child you can't do anything for yourself?"—was unanswered. On another occasion I related these comments to a group of parents and asked if they ever had this kind of experience. Most of them said they had and described people who wanted to do too much. When I asked how these situations might be handled a mother said, "It depends a lot on what they're doing and how you feel about it. The first mother you told about was mad because other people interfered and prevented her from doing her best. The second mother didn't want to be reminded all the time that she had a handicapped child. I think these problems would have to be handled in different ways."

"I'll tell you what I'd do about the one who kept sending cakes," suggested one of the mothers. "I'd bake a cake and send it to her every once in a while. That way she'd learn that I had time to bake, too!"

Some one else said with considerable feeling, "Or send her cakes back to her."

"You couldn't do that," someone objected. "Like was said, her heart's in the right place. Sending a cake back would be an insult. Instead of trying to be friendly she'd probably hate your child after that. You have to think about other people's feelings even though they're hurting yours."

"I think sending her a cake or some homemade jelly or something like that would be good," another member of the group affirmed. "But that's not enough. You should try to get to know her and let her get acquainted with your child. I think that would help her see things better. Maybe you could invite her to visit a clinic or a school with you."

I asked, "What about the ones who interfere with what you're doing?"

A mother replied, "Well, I certainly wish people would learn to ask, 'May I be of help?' or 'How can I help?' instead of just jumping in to do something."

Some one else added, "People are always offering to help when you don't need it and when you need help there's never anyone around."

"Yes, and then there are the advisors who don't try to do anything but are always telling us what to do," a mother chimed in. "You'd think they were doctors or had three of four handicapped children themselves."

After more comments of this type I said, "It seems that every parent of a handicapped child will meet this problem some-time or other. How can you best handle it?"

"You know I'd like to tell them to mind their own business," a mother began and then continued. "But I know we can't do that. Why make them feel bad when they really want to help. I guess one thing to do is to be sure you don't hurt their feel-ings if you can help it. To do that you'd better have your own feelings under control or you might just pop off and tell them to mind their own business before you realized what you were saying."

An older mother spoke up, "We've all been talking as if we never need any help. Let's face it honestly. Many parents of handicapped children need help at times. Shouldn't we figure out what kind of help we need? Then we could be ready to tell someone how to help when an offer was made. Maybe we could have in mind some little things which would satisfy them and not interfere with us too much. And I think we can all learn to say, 'No, thank you' in a way that it won't hurt people's feelings."

From these comments four suggestions for meeting the problems of over-acceptance may be summarized:

1. Recognize that some people are sincere in their desire to be of help and avoid rebuffing them.

Some people are genuinely concerned about handicapped children and their parents and want to be helpful. Unfortunately their efforts are often misguided and result in interference or give insult to the intended recipients of their aid. Snubbing of their offer will only hurt their feelings and perhaps create an attitude of non-acceptance of handicapped individuals.

2. Understand the nature of your own reactions.

It is natural for anyone to resent interference and try to prevent it. It is also natural for anyone to resent the kind of help which seems to say, "We know you can't do it but we can, so we'll help you." Even though such resentment is natural and expected it is not a satisfactory basis for making an effective response to an offer of assistance. When these feelings of resentment are recognized and understood it is easier to replace them with a concern about the feelings of other people. This latter concern provides a better basis for responding to offers of help.

3. Learn what kind of help you might use.

Parents sometimes cannot make effective use of offers of help because they have not analyzed their situation fully enough to know what to suggest. Questions such as—"What are the problems of getting a child in braces into a cab? How can one hold the attention of a hyperactive child?"—and the like should be thought through so an effective instruction can be given to a volunteering helper or, if no help is needed, the offer may be turned down courteously. Pre-planning of responses facilitates the handling of potentially trying situations.

4. *Try to redirect their efforts to your best advantage or to the best advantage of handicapped people in general.*

While it is true that people differ in their motives for offering help it is always safe to assume that a volunteer is genuinely interested in handicapped people. Obviously this interest should be nurtured. Even a polite, "No, thank you," may sometimes discourage this interest. In those cases it might be better to suggest some noninterfering thing to do such as, "Please hold the door." Or, "Would you like to take my package?" Overly-accepting people with whom parents have continuing contacts might be given appropriate literature to read, invited to visit a treatment or educational program, or encouraged to become members of a voluntary health program which is concerned with handicapped persons.

"What will people think?" Parents of handicapped children can't avoid the question but they can come to understand what prompts it and how they can deal with it effectively.

V

Those Flustered Feelings

Soon after they become aware of themselves as persons, children become prey to feelings of embarrassment. One can watch a young child playing, perfectly at ease, in the presence of company until his father or mother asks him to "say Humpty Dumpty for the folks." Immediately he seems to lose his composure. Perhaps he blushes and fidgets uneasily and acts as if he has forgotten the words, yet his parents know he has memorized them to perfection. With considerable urging and some prompting he stumbles through the verse. As soon as the guests have departed he can again render this rhyme without missing a syllable. His parents feel distressed and can't understand what happened to their ordinarily precocious child.

Have you ever been late for a party or meeting and had everyone stop talking and look at you as you walked into the room? Can you remember how you felt? Probably you felt your face grow warm and a kind of nervousness spread over you. Your thoughts were momentarily unsettled and you felt that you just wanted to slink way down in a back seat out of sight. After a bit you regained your composure. The nervousness subsided and your presence of mind returned.

Embarrassment Is a Reaction to Attention

Most people lose some of their poise if they are singled out for a compliment before a group of people, especially if it's unexpected. They blush, become nervous, find themselves at a loss for words, and in other ways show signs of embarrassment. Some of the pleasure at being complimented is lost because of the annoyance at being embarrassed.

A strikingly attractive coed once remarked that sometimes she wished she were not so pretty because it made her feel flustered to catch people looking at her. She said, "It's hard to keep your mind on what you're doing when you know that people are watching you. You just have to learn to ignore their staring but that's not always easy." Very similar comments were expressed by a teen-age boy whose surgically repaired cleft lip still bore a scar and there remained a noticeable break in the lip line. He said, "I wish people would quit looking at me. All the time I catch people's eyes on my face. It upsets me and my mind just goes blank. I'm getting mad about it and someday I'll up and bop somebody."

Embarrassment occurs often in our lives. It is a natural reaction anytime attention, either favorable or unfavorable, is focused on us. Certain physiological changes take place such as a rush of blood to the cheeks and neck and a generalized kind of nervousness. Some people perspire and report dryness of the mouth. Accompanying psychological changes include a loss of presence of mind, loss of poise, and a desire to escape. Most embarrassments pass quickly and are of little consequence in our lives. When they occur frequently we naturally become annoyed and even angry with those who embarrass us. If, for example, an individual complimented you frequently before the same group, you would soon be wishing he would stop it. If he continued, you would become annoyed and probably speak to him about it. Or, suppose that different people always embarrassed you in the same way as was the experience of the boy with a cleft lip. Your annoyance would grow each time you were embarrassed even though a different person might be involved each time.

Embarrassment Can Lead to Hostility

The natural reaction of embarrassment, which has such simple beginnings, can become quite complex and give rise to feelings of anger and hostility. We have seen a few parents whose feelings of embarrassment have grown malignantly into strong feelings of hostility toward anyone who directed attention to their child. Starting first with the natural, momentary loss of composure when they saw someone looking at their handicapped child, these parents, not understanding their feelings, eventually found themselves responding angrily to people who looked or asked questions. Such strong feelings, especially when not recognized and understood, rarely remain compartmentalized. Without the parents' being aware of what is happening they begin to react hostilely to professional workers who look at or ask about the handicapped child. Of course there are other reasons why parents might feel hostile toward professional workers, but these malevolent feelings which began as embarrassments can, like all hostility, constitute a barrier to communication and cooperation between parents and professional workers.

This development was seen in the remarks of a mother who participated in one of our small group discussion series. Her cerebral palsied child wore braces and received regular treatments at a clinic for crippled children. Talking about her feelings toward other people she said, "Boy, I sure told someone on the bus again today. There he sat, staring at Janie without a bit of shame. I am so sick and tired of it. Every day and every day it's the same thing. I just told him to turn around and mind his own business. Every time I see anyone looking at us anymore I tell them off. One of these days I'm going to tell those nosey therapists, too. Always wanting to know about this and about that. They'd better start minding their own business."

Another mother agreed, "People don't give any thought to your feelings at all. They look and look until it gets to be embarrassing. I think we parents have to do something to make them stop."

"I don't think you can make people stop," someone said, and then turning to Janie's mother asked, "Have you never looked at someone and wondered what was wrong with him?"

"Absolutely not! I wouldn't even think of doing such a thing," heatedly replied Janie's mother.

This outburst brought a stop to the comments for awhile.

Sensing that no one else was going to speak further on this topic I, as discussion leader, said, "I don't know about the rest of you but I look at people. I look at pretty girls, kids with freckles, people walking their dogs, people in uniforms, handicapped people—anyone who seems interesting. I don't stare but maybe I just steal a glance and sometimes I wonder about who they are and what they do. Maybe it's because of some curiosity I have that other people don't have."

Finding some support again, the woman who had questioned Janie's mother said, "Don't you think practically everyone has a lot of curiosity? I know I look at all the other children at the clinic and every time I see a handicapped person I try to watch him a little bit to see how he gets along. I often wonder about what his problem is and what caused it. Of course you don't need to stare but I don't see anything wrong with a glance. It seems natural to me."

Attention Is Often an Expression of Normal Curiosity
The parents fell to talking about natural curiosity and one by one they acknowledged looking at other people. All kinds of things attracted their attention: a woman's hat, an old man with a young wife, a boy on crutches, a man with big ears, a woman smoking on a bus. Someone mentioned seeing a man with a large birthmark on the side of his face and soon everyone was talking about birthmarks they had seen. Unaware of her contradiction, Janie's mother contributed to the discussion, "I saw a man one time. One half of his face was sorta red. I couldn't tell whether it was a burn or a birthmark. I wondered why he didn't do something to hide it." No one reminded her of her claim that she never looked at anyone and wondered

what was wrong with him but it was easier for her to talk about the problem after this discussion.

Curiosity is an ever present characteristic of human beings. Samuel Johnson wrote in *The Rambler:* "Curiosity is one of the permanent and certain characteristics of a vigorous mind." Its strength as a motivator is seen in Cowley's statement: "Curiosity, does, no less than devotion, pilgrims make." It begins with the infant's explorations of his environment and, unless it is killed, it lasts a lifetime. Man regards his curiosity as one of his most valued traits. Howe, writing at 87 years of age, implores Thieving Time in his poem of the same title:

> *Take what you must . . .*
> *Yet leave, O leave exempt from plunder*
> *My curiosity, my wonder!*

Parents of handicapped children must expect people's natural curiosity to be aroused by the difference of a handicapped child. Curiosity is not a bad word or undesirable trait. Of course, asking personal questions and rude staring will arouse indignation in anyone, but these are not to be confused with a normal interest or curiosity. Parents who have not learned to understand the embarrassment which wells up in them when someone's actions call attention to their handicapped child begin acting as if all curiosity is rude and must be stamped out.

Potential Embarrassment May Be Turned to Advantage

Continuing with our discussion session after Janie's mother told of looking at the man's birthmark, I asked, "Are there some things we can suggest doing which will help parents handle embarrassing situations?"

"Well I couldn't help but wonder how all those people feel when they are told to mind their own business," a mother responded. "I sat next to a one-armed man at dinner one time and admired how well he could manage with only one arm. I asked him how he had lost his arm and he said his dog bit it off. I felt like a fool and I hated him. I'll bet those people hate Mrs. Klare for telling them to mind their own business. Maybe they even hate Janie, too. In fact, they might even come to hate all handicapped kids."

Janie's mother said, "I never thought of it that way. But what can I do—they make me so mad!"

"That's just it. We've got to learn not to get mad. Maybe we should just ignore these people and not say anything at all," was one mother's proposal.

"Do you suppose we could bring up the subject in a nice way?" asked a mother. She continued, "Like when someone would be looking at Janie's braces Mrs. Klare could say, 'Hello, I see you noticed Janie's braces. She has cerebral palsy and I take her to the Crippled Children's Clinic twice a week for treatment. She's doing nicely.' Maybe that would open the door for a conversation."

This idea was picked up and amplified by another mother, "It would be a lot better than telling them to mind their own business. I think you're right, but we wouldn't want to stop and talk to everyone who looks at our children. Maybe when it's convenient like on a bus or in a waiting room we could make use of the opportunity to talk with people about handicapped children—not just our troubles but about handicapped children in general."

"I'm for that," another mother joined in. "I think we should do all we can to educate people about all types of handicapped children. Maybe the public will give us a little more support

61

if we keep telling everyone we can about what the problems are. Of course this means that we should be thinking about more than our own personal problems."

Embarrassment is a very common feeling which arises naturally when any kind of attention is focused on us. Often it is not serious and we can laugh about it. When aroused in connection with a handicapped child, however, the disturbance goes much deeper. Repeated embarrassments, regardless of their depth, can result in resentment which over time can develop into anger and hostility. Some ways parents and others have suggested for handling the embarrassments which come from people's curiosity about handicapped children are:

1. Recognize your embarrassment and how it affects your behavior.

Embarrassment has certain physiologic and psychologic characteristics which, when present, interfere with rational behavior. Responses made when one is nervous and lacking in presence of mind are likely to be undesirable responses. Parents should learn to check their embarrassment or wait until the peak of physiologic and psychologic change has passed before responding to a source of embarrassment. A delayed response will probably be less emotionally toned than a response made in the heat of embarrassment.

2. Recognize that most people are naturally curious.

Much of man's progress has resulted from his curiosity about everything he sees. Anything different is likely to attract his attention. This means that handicapped children will come under the observation of many people. Parents are likely to call this observation "staring" and react to what they think the behavior is rather than what the other person intended it to be. Parents of handicapped children themselves have considerable curiosity about other people. Identifying evidences of their own curiosity may help parents become more tolerant of curiosity in others.

3. Become aware that some embarrassing situations may be of your own making.

Parents of handicapped children sometimes become hypersensitive about anything having to do with their handicapped child. They unconsciously look for evidences that other people are staring at them or talking about them. With their minds set in this way, their imaginations are apt to play tricks on them and they become embarrassed for no good cause. Also embarrassment sometimes arises because parents put their handicapped children into situations for which they are not ready. When what seems like a "catastrophe" occurs the parents become embarrassed.

4. Operate on the philosophy that parents of handicapped children should function as public relations representatives for all handicapped persons.

Parents of handicapped children have an especially important role as good-will ambassadors for all handicapped persons. Realizing that their reactions to incidents relating to their own handicapped child might rebound unfavorably on other handicapped people, parents should become sensitive to the feelings of others and avoid offending them. Whenever possible they should turn potentially embarrassing situations into opportunities for furthering public education concerning the interests of handicapped persons.

Following these suggestions will not mean that one will never be embarrassed again. Embarrassment usually comes on us unexpectedly and hence, cannot always be guarded against. Attention to these suggestions will reduce the number of times embarrassing incidents arise relating to your handicapped child and will help prevent embarrassment from developing into anger and hostility.

VI

Who's to Blame?

Man has always wondered about his world. He has tried to explain to himself why things happen as they do. A recent cartoon, poking fun at people who attribute today's violent weather to atomic explosions, shows two cave men standing in the mouth of their cave looking out at a heavy downpour. One says to the other, "We didn't have storms like this before people started shooting those bows and arrows." We can chuckle at this but it points up nicely that man has always tried to find an explanation for why things happen. Often his explanations are quite farfetched. It's hardly conceivable today that people could have explained the sun's apparent movement across the daytime sky by believing it was a golden chariot driven by a god. This was the way the early Greeks and Romans explained the sun to themselves. They knew about chariots so, naturally, they described the sun in terms of something familiar. The American Indians, not knowing about chariots, believed the sun was a god holding a drawn bow thus making it appear round. Today we know the sun is a star about 1,3000,000 times as large as the earth, located at the center of our solar system. The earth and several other planets travel in orbits around the sun. Because of a continuing nuclear reaction inside the sun, energy flows to the outside making the surface temperature about 10,800 degrees Fahrenheit. An astronomer writing today could fill a book with information about the sun. With his telescopes, spectroscopes, radio telescopes, rocket probes, and many other modern devices he has learned much about the sun. At the same time men have been learning many things about the world and other planets. He has seen gases burn in his laboratory and learned that different elements give off different patterns of light. When he analyzes the light from a star he can compare the patterns with his laboratory patterns and identify the elements of which the star is made. Modern man is still explaining the sun in terms of what he knows but his information now goes far beyond chariots and bows and arrows.

Experiences Determine Explanations

It is natural, then, for man to try to explain things on the basis of his experience using the information he has at hand. This phenomenon is often seen in the explanations parents work out to account for the birth of a handicapped child. For a number of years I have included this question in my conferences with parents of handicapped children: "It's pretty natural for parents to wonder what might have caused their child's problem. Can you tell me some of the things you have thought about?" Always parents offer explanations based on the information available to them. Often it is "chariot" or "bow-and-arrow" type information. Only occasionally is it twentieth century information.

At a cleft-palate clinic I was talking to the young parents of a child recently born with a cleft of the lip and palate. As usual, I asked if they had any ideas about what might have caused it. The mother blushed and hesitated. Finally, her husband said, "Go ahead, honey, tell him about it." His wife went on to explain that during the last weeks of her pregnancy she would spend most of each evening reading in bed. Her husband would lie beside her reading mystery stories which made him nervous so, while reading, he picked his teeth with his fingernail. Just a few nights before the baby was born she became so annoyed with her husband's teeth picking that she slapped him causing his nail to cut his lip. As a result of her annoyance, her baby was born with a cleft lip. This explanation is as reasonable as the Greek's description of the sun as a golden chariot. She used the information she had to explain why things happened as they did. She was unaware that microscopic studies of embryos had shown that by the end of the third month after conception the development of the human face is completed. Nothing occurring after that time can produce a cleft or eliminate one that remains after the period of facial development has passed. No more than could the ancients talk about the sun in terms of incandescent gases could she explain that her baby's cleft lip was the result of failure of union of the mesoderm of the maxillary and frontonasal processes. But there is a significant difference between her situation and that of the Greeks. There was nowhere in the world better information about the sun than the Greeks had. On the other hand, professional workers possess much more information about the nature and causes of disabling conditions than parents do. From them parents can expect to get help in understanding the possible causes of their children's problems.

On another occasion I was talking with the parents of a severely retarded mongoloid child. These children usually have some distinctive physical characteristics. Their eyes appear to slant, the bridge of the nose is often flattened, and there are many other features which are present in varying combinations. The child whom we were discussing possessed many of the stigmata associated with the condition and, to even a casual observer, was noticeably different in appearance from other children. In response to my inquiry about what the parents considered likely causes, the mother said that the month before their child was born she had worn a Halloween costume and taken her other children out for tricks and treats. Then when they came home she went to a masquerade party with her husband.

"All around me were those funny faces," she said, "and when I got home I just threw my costume over the foot of the bed and went right to sleep. All night I kept dreaming of false faces. I never should have done it because that's why the baby looks the way he does."

This is no more absurd than thinking the sun is a god with a drawn bow. She could not know that researchers are certain that the interference which produces mongolism must occur very early in the period of embryologic development. They can tell this from the parts of the body which are affected. Nor could she know that researchers in Great Britain have found an extra chromosome in the tissues of mongoloid children. This means that at the time of conception the mongoloid child's development began with 47 instead of the usual 46 chromosomes. From that instant on, the die was cast and nothing the mother did or didn't do could change things. Of course she couldn't know this any more than the Indians could know the scientific facts about the sun, so both she and the Indians made "bow-and-arrow" explanations of what they observed.

Parents Blame Themselves

In a sense parents are like primitive people when they try to explain to themselves why their child is handicapped. The only information available to them is unscientific information so they naturally come up with unscientific explanations. This is not to say that today's scientists know all about the causes of handicapping conditions any more than they know all about the sun. They have learned a lot, though, and are rapidly learning more. It is no longer adequate or necessary to employ primitive ideas or superstitions to explain why handicapping conditions occur. This point was well made by a mother at a meeting of parents of children with cleft palates. The group decided to talk about the causes of their children's handicaps.

One mother began, "I think you can want a child too much. We had two boys and my husband and I desperately wanted a girl. Because we had so much wanted a girl and didn't want any more boys, we were given a boy with a cleft palate."

Another mother said, "I know exactly what you mean. We

had two girls and felt just the way you did so we got a girl with a deformed mouth. It isn't right to want a boy or a girl too much."

There was much discussion of this type with various mothers attributing their child's condition to something she had thought or done. Finally an older woman, who had been listening quietly, began in a tentative manner, "It seems that you are all saying that God gave you a handicapped child because of something you have thought or done. I wonder if it's fair to blame God for our children's handicaps. If he wanted to punish us, I think he would do it directly and not punish little children. People a long time ago used to blame God for everything—famines, plagues, floods. Everything they didn't understand they said was God's way of punishing them. When men learned more about farming, they learned how to prevent famines. Doctors now know what causes diseases so we don't have plagues like they did in olden times. Today we are building dams to control floods. Now we don't have to blame God for famines, plagues, and floods because we know more about them. When we don't understand what causes something, it's natural to think that there's a supernatural reason for it."

Probably one of the main reasons early man invented gods was to help him explain things that happened. Desirable events occurred when his gods were pleased and, when man incurred the displeasure of one of his gods, unpleasant or disastrous events transpired. We have carried some of these beliefs down to present times. Their influence could be seen in the attitude of the mother of a cerebral palsied girl when she told me, "I guess I don't have to think very hard to know why I have a handicapped daughter. I was no angel when I was young. I lived it up plenty. Now God is making me pay for my sins and He's seeing to it that my daughter won't do the things I did."

There is considerable similarity between early man's concept of "displeasing" his gods and modern man's concept of sinning. Both concepts carry the expectation that punishment will be meted out for the wrongdoings—and who has not done wrong sometime in his life? Ovid's opinion of his fellow men in this regard is expressed in his lines:

If Jove a thunderbolt should hurl whene'er men sin,
His armoury would quickly empty be.

The New Testament suggests that no stones were thrown when the crowd was admonished: "He that is without sin among you, let him first cast a stone at her." Any person who has a handicapped child can easily recall some wrongdoing in his past for which he might be punished if he wants to put the blame for his child's condition on God. Considering man's natural tendency to ascribe to supernatural forces any events he cannot otherwise explain, his expectation to be punished for his wrongdoings, and the fact that all of us can recall some wrongdoings of our past, it is not surprising that guilt feelings are so easily aroused. As parents have come to understand the nature of their children's conditions and learned that scientific investigations have shed much light on the cause of these problems, they have recognized the inadequacy of their self-incriminating explanations.

Sometimes parents blame themselves in other ways, thinking they may have done something which is directly responsible for their child s problem. We often find a mother, for example, who is sure that a fall which occurred during her pregnancy is the cause of her child's difficulty. A good refutation of this was given by a mother in one of the group discussions. She had listened to three or four mothers describe their falls and tell how they just knew that the fall was the cause of their child's condition.

"I don't believe it," she exploded. "I had a bad fall at seven months and my mother-in-law said that's why our boy is so slow in everything. She said I probably tore his nerves loose from his brain or something. It made me so mad that I started asking all the mothers I knew if they ever fell when they were pregnant. Practically all of them had. How come, then, they don't have crippled children? You mothers all know that a baby is protected inside a sac of water. If the sac doesn't break I don't see how the baby could be hurt by a fall. We gotta quit blaming ourselves for all these things and not let other people put the blame on us either."

At a clinic for handicapped children I saw several times during a four-year period a mother with an unusual explanation of how she caused her son's problem. There could be no doubt that he was grossly mentally retarded. At 6 he could barely do the things expected of a 2-year-old, yet his mother could not accept the diagnosis of mental deficiency and apparently found it difficult to cooperate with the clinic staff. She persistently demanded therapy which the doctors didn't feel was indicated and was generally disagreeable when anyone tried to talk with her. During our fifth or sixth conference she asked me if there were any ways to determine if a child had pressure on the brain. I told her there were and suggested that we discuss them with the clinic physician. She seemed reluctant to talk with the doctor about it so I said, "You've been thinking something might have happened to cause pressure on Mark's brain and you'd like to find out about it sometime. Is that it?"

She began to cry and said, "I'm not sure if I want to find out or not." Then she told me this story. Shortly after she was settled in her hospital room her doctor examined her and said it would be some time before the baby would be delivered and that he would be back soon. The nurse, after giving her instructions to ring if she needed anything, left with the doctor. A short time later, the mother, feeling she needed to go to the bathroom and not wanting to bother the nurse, arose from the bed and went to the toilet. There she delivered her baby into the toilet bowl. This story was so repulsive to her that she couldn't bring herself to tell it yet, ever since she became aware that her child was not learning well, she had felt that his head had been injured on the sides of the bowl. When he heard of the mother's concern the clinic physician arranged for an X-ray study of Mark's head to be made. As he expected, the results were negative, but the procedure gave Mark's mother the reassurance she needed that his head had not been injured in his unusual delivery.

Self-Blame Influences Parental Attitudes

Occasionally a parent will ask, "Why are you interested in what we think caused the problem? Isn't that a personal matter?" The story of Mark's mother illustrates very well why professional people are interested in what parents regard as the cause of their child's condition and how they answer the question—"Who is to blame?" Their beliefs concerning cause and responsibility can have a definite influence on how much understanding of their child's difficulty they can develop and how they react to professional people. As long as Mark's mother thought she was responsible for his condition her mind was closed to everything else. Not until she had talked through this problem and received reassurance that she was not to blame did she really open her mind to what the professional people were trying to say to her. Like Mark's mother, parents sometimes carry around such a heavy weight of guilt that it depresses their feelings and colors all their thinking about their child's problems. Professional workers need to understand these feelings if they are to help parents.

Doctors Are Handy Targets

In addition to God and themselves, parents have only their doctors left to blame for their child's handicap and one can almost predict that in any parent-centered group discussion where parents feel free to talk, the doctors will be subjected to a round of criticism and accusation. Often, even those parents who blame either God or themselves feel that their child would have been all right if only the doctor had not failed them in some way. These excerpts from parent's discussions illustrate how some parents felt about the doctor who delivered their child or who provided his early medical care.

The mother of a child with cerebral palsy voiced an oft-mentioned complaint. "He got there too late. The baby was practically born and the only one around was a nurse. He knew I was pregnant for months, so surely you'd think he'd plan to be at the hospital on time. If he'd only been there I think things would be different."

By some parents, the doctor's use of medications is criticized as in these remarks made by the mother of a mentally retarded child. "Why did he give me that medicine? I was so groggy that I didn't know what was going on. He can't tell me that this didn't have something to do with it. I know I wanted a little but he gave me too much."

Fathers, particularly, complain that the doctors won't tell them anything; however, mothers also mention this point. One father grumbled, "Our doctor wouldn't tell us anything. You'd think it wasn't even our child the way he put us off when we asked any questions. I figured right away that something must have gone wrong and he wanted to hide it." This father was speaking the thoughts of many parents.

A common charge parents of handicapped children level at the doctor who provides postnatal care is seen in these words of a young mother: "I kept telling the doctor something was wrong with Mary Sue, but he would tell me that I was just over-anxious and that the baby was all right. When I saw she wasn't learning to sit up I asked him what was wrong with her and he said that some babies are just a little slower than others but that I shouldn't worry. When she was 18 months old and still wasn't sitting up I took her to another doctor who said right away that she had cerebral palsy."

At most discussion sessions there are some parents whose comments help the group understand the feelings parents of handicapped children sometimes develop toward their doctors. These excerpts from various discussion sessions summarize their important points.

"I think one of the reasons we blame our doctors is because we expect too much of them." The father of an adolescent cerebral palsied boy was speaking. "Before I got to know any doctors personally I thought they were all gods who knew everything. Now I know that they are highly trained men who are devoted to helping people. They try to do their best but sometimes their best just isn't good enough. And another reason is that we act like we're their only patient. I belong to a club with a couple of doctors and they're so busy we hardly get to see them. I don't see how they can give us all the personal attention we'd like to have but when they don't, we get mad at them."

"I know I was real mad at my doctor and thought it was all his fault because he didn't get there in time," a mother told the group. "I used to think some terrible things about him. When our boy was about three years old we learned that all his problems came from the measles I had when I was about two months pregnant. Here, he would have been born the same way whether the doctor got there on time or not. Long before he was born his trouble started and there wasn't anything any doctor could do about it. Then I felt bad because I had blamed him so unjustly."

"I suppose one reason we blame the doctor is because we need a scapegoat," another mother suggested. "Whenever something goes wrong we have to blame somebody and the doctor is a convenient person to put the blame on. He's the one in charge when the baby is born and it's natural for us to make him bear the blame because things didn't turn out right."

It is probably true that parents have no more justification for blaming their doctor than they have for blaming God or themselves when their child is born with a handicap. Perhaps a doctor might sometimes make an error in judgment, but, if he does, it is a human error for which he hardly deserves parental condemnation. Such errors would account for only a very small fraction of the children born with handicaps. Investigators are finding that many handicapping conditions are the result of such prenatal factors as defective genes, bio-chemical disturbances, and other problems which medical science has not yet learned to control. Even today it is often not possible to determine exactly what caused a child's handicap. Under these circumstances, attempts to blame the doctor for a child's problem are based, as one father put it," more on emotion than on reason."

At a meeting of fathers and mothers someone suggested talking about how parents could overcome their tendency to want to find out who was to blame for their having a handicapped child. After several parents had expressed themselves, a father said, "I think we should quit thinking about God or some person as the cause and think more about physical conditions which might have caused it. And, suppose we do find out what caused it—what can we do about it? Some people spend so much time worrying about who's to blame for their kid's problem that they don't think enough about what they can do about it."

"It's not only the time you spend worrying about who's to blame," added a mother. "If you think you're to blame or that God's punishing you, you're so heartsick that it's hard to make yourself think of anything else."

A father who was a farmer said, "I know you might not like to compare children with cows but I think we can learn a lot from animals. Every once in a while we get a poor calf. Nobody says, 'Who's to blame?' We just know that something went wrong. The veterinarian says a calf starts from one cell which divides to make two, the two to make four, and so on until there are millions of cells in a newborn calf. This process is very complicated and you got to expect that something will go wrong sometimes. Babies are a lot more complex than calves so something can go wrong with them, too, when all these cells start dividing."

"When I read someplace that almost 150,000 mentally subnormal children are born each year in the United States, I quit looking for someone to blame for our child's retardation," a mother commented. "It didn't seem to me that all those children could have had poor doctors or that their parents had done something wrong. I began to realize that just like germs and viruses can cause diseases after children are born, maybe they can cause things to go wrong before a child is born. We don't blame ourselves when our children get mumps and measles. Why should we blame ourselves if something happens to them before they are born?"

Another parent brought the discussion of this topic to a close by saying, "I've learned tonight that one thing parents can do to straighten themselves out on the question of who is to blame is to talk about it. I know I learned a lot from this discussion that I'd never thought about before. When you keep these questions inside you, your thinking gets into a rut. Talking about them makes you think about them in different ways."

These suggestions for changing parents' feelings about the question—"Who's to blame?"—may be summarized as follows:
1. Change the question from "Who is to blame?" to "What might have caused it?"
Handicapping conditions are caused by physical events, not

by people. Concentration on fixing the blame for their child's condition creates an unwholesome emotional state for parents. An objective inquiry into possible causal factors, on the other hand, leads parents away from emotionally based personal condemnations. If the cause of a handicapping condition is to be found, it will be through intellectual rather than emotional approaches. From the handicapped child's point of view, an even more important question than "What caused it?" is "What can be done about it?" Actually, determination of the cause is of more interest to scientific investigators than it is to persons engaged in habilitating the handicapped for they have to work with the child regardless of what the cause might be.

2. Find out as much as you can about what science has learned about the condition.

As man learned more and more about his world, he less frequently had to explain the cause of events in terms of supernatural intervention. And it is so with handicapping conditions just as with any other natural phenomena. Today there is probably not a single physical condition of man which is not receiving the attention of some investigator. Concerning many conditions, much is known, while the study of some others is just beginning. Parents who familiarize themselves with what scientists have learned about the handicapping condition of concern to them will be less apt to blame God, themselves, or their doctor for their child's problem.

3. Discuss fully with some trusted professional person your thoughts about possible causes.

Often parents are upset because on clinic day they get short answers from the doctor to such questions as, "What caused it?" Usually the answers are short because an adequate discussion of the topic would require more time than is available if all the scheduled patients are to be seen. Also, the general atmosphere on a busy clinic day is rarely appropriate for the discussion os such personal questions as, "Who is to blame?" Rapport between professional worker and parent is important in developing an objective point of view about possible causes. Parents who are troubled about blame and cause can expect the greatest help from private conferences with a professional worker in whom they have confidence or through discussions with other parents under a qualified leader.

We have seen that self-blame is a very natural reaction for parents when a handicapped child is born. When viewed this way no one—parents and professional persons alike—should be surprised if parents reproach themselves and feel that they are at fault for what went wrong. There is nothing darkly terrible about a parent's blaming himself because he doesn't have enough information to think more objectively about possible causes. But as soon as the labels "guilt" or "guilt feeling" become attached to this normal parental reaction, everyone—again parents and professional persons alike—assume that the parent is possessed of a devil which must be cast out. Of course, guilt feelings can at times be powerful forces in affecting behavior. Probably this is why the term has taken on such sinister connotations for both lay and some professional people. The popular concept of guilt suggests that it is deeply abnormal for anyone to have guilt feelings, in other words, to blame himself. How, though, can it be abnormal for parents, the main characters in the act of procreation, to feel responsible for the condition of their offspring? In the absence of scientific information they naturally look to themselves as the source of the trouble. Self-blame—call it "guilt feeling," if you will—is a normal reaction. It creates problems for parents only when it persists and interferes with their most important job—doing all that is possible to habilitate the handicapped child.

Evaluation Can Arouse Guilt Feelings

Occasionally professional workers will unwittingly arouse guilt feelings in self-critical parents. Often during an evaluation, parents will be asked some question such as, "Where was your child evaluated before?" Or, "What have you been told about Johnny's problem?" Parents who have not had their child examined previously sometimes interpret these questions to mean that they should have been doing something about the child's problem long before this. Their feeling that they have been neglectful is intensified by the professional emphasis on the importance of early diagnosis and early treatment. Unless the child's condition can be corrected completely, these parents are often plagued by the thought that it might have been corrected or at least the child might have done better, if only they had gotten help for him sooner. At a discussion meeting a mother was belaboring herself for failing to take her deaf child to a doctor earlier.

"Maybe he could have done something to save her hearing," she bewailed.

Another mother started her on the road to peace of mind with these comments. "You said you went as soon as you felt pretty sure something was wrong, didn't you? I don't see what more you can ask of yourself. Parents certainly can't go running to the doctor the instant they first suspect something is wrong with a child. You have to watch the child for a little while so you can tell the doctor what to look for."

Even those parents who delay going to a doctor because they are afraid of what they might learn about their child seldom procrastinate long enough to reduce significantly the level of achievable habilitation. The parental desire to do what is best for their child is far greater than their fear of receiving bad news.

Actually the question about previous examinations is asked of most parents whether or not the person taking the history thinks any particular child should have been examined earlier. The only intention of the questioner is to obtain a complete history and it is unfortunate that sometimes the questions cause parental self-blame.

Another inadvertent contribution of professional people to the guilt feelings of parents is seen in the following experience. One day I observed a physician and physical therapist evaluating a cerebral palsied child who was on a home treatment program with the mother doing the exercises under the supervision of the therapist. The physician, partly to check up but largely to make conversation, said to the mother, "Do you give him his exercises every day?"

The mother replied with a hesitant Yes.

The doctor continued with his examination and the therapist said to him, "I see Sammy once a month and his mother is supposed to exercise him a half hour a day. Isn't that right, Mrs. Baldwood?"

Again the mother hesitated and finally gave a noticeably unsure Yes.

As she left the therapist reminded her, "Be sure to keep up those exercises, now!"

Noting that she seemed troubled, I went out with her and

said, "I noticed that you didn't seem quite sure about how much exercise you give Sammy. Have you had difficulty following the schedule?"

Mrs. Baldwood began to cry and said, "I'm a poor mother. No wonder Sammy doesn't get better faster. I know I slip up on those exercises sometimes." Then she went on to tell how one day the telephone rang in the midst of the exercises and she never got back to them. On another occasion a neighbor dropped in for coffee before the half hour was up. During the past summer she had missed several days when relatives were visiting and again when the family went to a fair. She said, "I try to give him those exercises every day for a half hour but sometimes I just can't get to it. If I want Sammy to get better I guess I'll have to put his exercises first."

Without meaning to do so, and unaware of what had happened, the professional workers had made Mrs. Baldwood feel that Sammy was not making as much progress as they expected and that she was responsible. Actually, they don't know that a half hour is better than 20 or 25 minutes. Nor do they know that the exercises must be given seven days a week instead of five to be effective. What they mean is that all the prescribed exercises should be given regularly. There is really nothing magical about "a full half hour" of treatment or an unvarying seven-day-a-week routine. These are guides from which the professional workers expect parents to deviate occasionally. Most parents try to carry out programs as instructed. The few who pay no attention to instructions are usually not bothered by the comments of therapists or doctors. Unfortunately the most conscientious parents are also the most easily hurt. Professional workers are becoming increasingly aware of the impact even their causal questions and comments might have on the feelings of parents. Before blaming themselves, it is a good rule for parents to ask professional workers to clarify any comments or questions which parents find disturbing. Many parents will naturally feel reluctant to talk with doctors, therapists, teachers, and other professional workers about such problems. However, frank inquiries about potentially disturbing matters will result in better mental hygiene for the parents and the improved intercommunication will help the professionals increase their effectiveness.

VII

Worry, Worry, Worry

In *The Story of Mankind,* van Loon says of the great-great grandfather of the human race:

> *During the hours of the day, this primitive human being prowled about looking for things to eat. When night descended upon the earth, he hid his wife and his children in a hollow tree behind some heavy boulders, for he was surrounded on all sides by ferocious animals and when it was dark these animals began to prowl about, looking for something to eat . . . . It was a world where you must either eat or be eaten, and life was very unhappy because it was full of fear and misery.*

And here we have the suggestion that even before the dawn of history man was concerned about himself and his children.

Whether or not he was yet intelligent enough to worry about such matters as hunger and safety, it appears that he was moved by some strong drive to provide for them. His first provisions were simple—a hollow tree or a cave for protection, some berries or raw meat for food. As man developed, however, he soon recognized that his needs and those of his children could best be met through planning which considered future as well as immediate needs. Security, the basic purpose of long-range planning, was incompatible with a nomadic existence, so history finds man's life taking on an agricultural pattern. With an eye to future needs man learned to produce more than enough food for his immediate needs and developed methods of preserving and storing surpluses for use in times of famine.

Man's deep and universal concern about the question—"What of the future?"—has led to the development of such protective devices as life insurance, savings accounts, annuities, investment programs, pensions, retirement programs, and the like. During the first quarter of this century the majority of European nations, members of the British Empire, and several South American republics adopted systems of compulsory old-age insurance to assure a happy answer to at least the financial aspect of the question—"What of the future?" In the United States the security-threatening depression of the thirties gave rise to many plans for assisting those in need of support and in 1935 a social security law was enacted which has come to provide benefits for the aged, the disabled, and a worker's survivors.

Yes, man has come a long way since security was provided by a hollow tree and hunger satisfied by a piece of raw meat. But he has not lost his concern about the future. Since its first enactment the social security program of the United States has undergone a number of revisions each designed to enlarge or extend the benefits. The Englishman's concern about his future recently led the government of Great Britain to develop a program so inclusive that it was characterized as giving "womb to tomb" protection.

The Future Is Everyone's Concern

With this long history what can be more natural than one's concern about the future? As Charles Kettering remarked: "We should all be concerned about the future because we will have to spend the rest of our lives there." Natural concern about how their children will spend their future lives is the seed from which much parental worry and anxiety develop. When the child's future is darkened by a disability, parental concern quickly takes on the emotional overtones characteristic of chronic worry. The universality of this concern is noted by Earl Miers when he writes in the introduction to the booklet, *Building an Estate for a Crippled Child:* "Parents know. In quiet moments, the question is there. *What then?*" The authors of the booklet say it, too, in another way. They open their discussion with these words:

> *"If anything should happen to me, who will look out for Joe?" "When we are gone, who will take care of Mary?" This nagging fear haunts every father and mother with a child who lacks the strength to make his way in the world without full or partial help.*

Financial security for their handicapped child is but one aspect of parental concern about his future. Another concern arises from man's inborn drive to progress. Ever since man appeared on the earth each succeeding generation has possessed a little more knowledge and a little greater skill than its predecessor. Civilization developed because of man's desire to add to what had been learned in the past. Man expects each generation to produce better housing, improved transportation, quicker communication, better food and clothing, more knowledge about the universe, and so on. Individual man—parents—carry this expectation also. Each parent seems to hope that his children will reach a higher rung on the ladder of success than he himself attained. Parents want their children to have better educations, get better jobs, enjoy a richer standard of living, improve their social status; in other words, to progress as a family. Again, these are natural parental aspirations with roots dating back to the beginning of man. For these aspirations to be realized today, however, a child must be able to learn to walk, talk, write, read, think, and perform many other tasks which are difficult or impossible for some severely handicapped children. When parents realize that their child's disability will prevent him from developing satisfactory skills of ambulation, communication, or thinking, they very naturally feel that the family's advance up the ladder of success has been halted. Not only are they concerned for themselves but they worry about their child's inability to contribute to the general progress of society and to make a place for himself.

Providing a future for the severely handicapped child often cannot be defined in such modern terms as education and a good job. Rather, the family is forced to revert to planning for protection and providing for hunger. Such care they expect to provide for all children during infancy, but the pattern of normal development is from dependence to independence. Self-sufficiency is regarded as a major characteristic of the mature individual. In fact, it is generally expected that not only will our children be able to provide for themselves when they grow up but also that they can help support their parents if need be. Recognition that a handicapped child's development will not progress beyond a dependent state strikes a terrible blow at parents' concept of how life should be. Under these circumstances, is it any wonder that parents of disabled children worry about the future?

Child Care Raises Basic Questions

A group of parents of severely involved cerebral palsied children decided one evening to discuss what worried them most. The first speaker, a father, set the tone for the other parents when he said, "I worry about what the future holds for John. Right now he can't walk, or talk, or feed himself. Of course he's only 6-years-old and we keep hoping, but we know in our hearts that he will never be able to take care of himself. What will happen to him after we're gone?"

Another father interrupted, "What do you mean after you're gone? What makes you think you'll always be able to take care of him while you are here? I live in fear that I might have a stroke or a heart attack or an accident that will disable me. Then my wife will not only have our boy to take care of all by herself but she'll have my care as an extra burden. You don't have to die to make it difficult to provide care for a handicapped child."

A mother spoke up, "Fathers aren't the only ones who worry about who will take care of the child. A couple of years ago I had a broken leg and couldn't get around for several weeks. We had an awful time getting anyone to take care of Nancy. My husband had to miss work. Neighbors dropped in to help but didn't like feeding a big girl and taking her to the bathroom and all that. Things were sure hectic until I got on my feet again. I get sick with worry every time I get a little ache or pain because I'm so afraid I might get laid up again. What Stan would do if anything serious happened to me, I don't know. We could afford to hire someone to help with Nancy but where can you find someone to look after a handicapped child day in and day out? It's not like nursing someone who's going to get better some day."

John's father spoke up again, "We worry about that part of it, too. I have a lot of life insurance with John as my beneficiary and now he can get social security disability benefits if I die or retire or become disabled. We don't worry so much about the money part anymore. What bothers us is *who* will take care of him."

"We have that part worked out," a mother said seriously. "Our older daughter says she will take care of Laurie if anything happens to her dad or me. Eleanore just loves her little sister and helps me take care of her all the time. She says when she gets married she wants to live near us so she can take Laurie when we aren't here anymore."

"I don't think that's a good solution at all," a mother spoke out. "In the first place, what if something happens to Eleanore? Suppose she gets sick or has an accident shortly after you pass on? Who will take care of Laurie then? Or what if she dies?"

A father added, "We've thought about all this, too. We have

an older daughter and we want her to get an education and lead her own life. We don't think it would be fair to make her spend her life taking care of a handicapped brother when she could be a teacher or a nurse or something. And, like you say, even if we did want her to take care of her brother, what assurance would we have that she wouldn't become disabled or die?"

"That's right," remarked a mother who was separated from her husband. "And even if she did want to take care of her sister her husband might not like the idea. My husband's whole attitude changed when we learned Myra had cerebral palsy. It just seemed that he couldn't take the responsibility or something. After he left I had to go back to live with my parents. I don't know what I'd do if they weren't here."

"I hadn't thought about it that way," Laurie's mother said. "I read that in China the members of a family looked after each other. When the parents get old their children support them and if they're sick they take care of them. This book said they don't need poor houses or old folks homes or anything like that in China. I don't see why families can't take care of themselves here just the same."

"Because we have a different culture," explained a father. "In China there was very little industry. Most everything was made at home or in a little village. People didn't travel around very much. The parents picked the husbands and wives for their children. Young men were expected to follow in their father's footsteps, learn his trade, and never question anything he said. All this attitude kept China a backward country for centuries.

I think unreasonable family ties and strong parental domina-
tion of children stifle progress. I don't think we'd want this
philosophy in America."

"That's my point of view, too," agreed another father. "A
friend of mine had an older brother who had spinal meningitis
when he was a baby. It left him blind and mentally sub-normal. After his dad died my friend had to stay around home a
lot to help his mother take care of his brother who couldn't
feed himself or go to the bathroom. In fact, he hardly even
knew anyone. My friend expected to stay at home all his life
helping his mother but during his last year of high school his
brother died. My friend went to college and then studied to be
a doctor. Now, which would be better for society: for him to
have stayed home to help his mother care for a mentally defective brother, or for him to become a doctor? I think that
caring for disabled children is the responsibility of society as
a whole not just the responsibility of a family which happened
to have a misfortune."

Laurie's mother spoke anxiously, "I guess all I can do is
hope Laurie passes away before I do. I don't know what will
happen if she doesn't."

This sobering remark brought a lull in the discussion. Each
parent was occupied with his own thoughts. Ordinarily I would
have encouraged them to discuss their feelings about the hope
expressed by Laurie's mother that Laurie would pass away
first, but this was the last session scheduled for this group and
it seemed better to guide them back to their discussion of planning for the future. "Many parents have expressed this same
hope," I said. "The severely handicapped child's passing on before the parents seems to be such a perfect solution to the care

problem that I suppose practically all parents have had this thought cross their minds. This solution, though, is in the hands of Fate. We have no control over who will pass away first so we can't base all our plans on this possibility. Suppose you were planning a program for the future care of your handicapped child. What things would you be sure to provide?"

"Adequate care would be the first essential," a father suggested. "This would include everything — looking after his health, giving him his treatments, good food, schooling, recreation . . . ."

"Wouldn't that depend on what the child needed?" asked a mother. "Not all children would need physical therapy or speech therapy. They wouldn't all be able to benefit from schooling. Everyone would need certain basic things like health care, good food, and some type of recreation. After these, there's not much point in demanding therapy if a child doesn't need it or work on reading and writing if he's too retarded to learn them."

The first father replied, "I suppose that what I mean is that the handicapped person should be able to live in dignity. This means that all his needs would be provided for and that he would continue to be an individual and not just a number or a patient."

Another parent suggested, "After our earlier discussion, I would think that guaranteed continuity of care would be important to all of us. We were saying that you couldn't be sure that brothers and sisters would be able to give continuing care. We asked what would happen if the sister became disabled or died. The same kind of question might be asked about a privately operated home or school. What happens if the owner can't work or if there aren't enough children enrolled to pay expenses. It looks to me as if the kind of guaranteed continuity of care we want can best be provided in a home supported in some way by the government."

The pros and cons of government supported programs were discussed with the dangers of bureaucracy getting considerable attention. The parent who had suggested a government supported home finally asked, "If we are so opposed to bureaucracy and to government support why do we use the public schools, the courts, and the roads. They are all supported by public funds and administered by bureaucrats. Why should I accept public help for the education of my normal children and reject it for my handicapped child? If we followed the argument that we don't want government help because you can't trust politicians and the government's getting too strong, we'd soon have to go back to living in caves!"

"Another thing we haven't talked about is the cost of providing the kind of program we want," a mother proposed. "We don't have much money and we're worried about how we can provide for our girl's future with the little bit of money we have."

"Well, I guess most of us are in that fix," another mother agreed.

"Caring for a handicapped child is expensive because it's required over a long time," a mother noted. "You can get hospital insurance to help with operations and insurance to help with medical expense but I don't know of any help you can get for long-term care of a severely handicapped child."

"That's all the more reason for having state supported schools and homes for severely handicapped persons," came back the proponent of government help. "The cost should be shared by all citizens, not borne alone by parents of handicapped children. Look at all we said we wanted in a program designed to provide future care for our children: adequate care, an opportunity to live with dignity, guaranteed continuity, and low cost. The only way I can see to get all these is through a program supported and operated by the state."

"I don't see how people can live with dignity in a state home," Laurie's mother objected. "They are so big and impersonal. They're just like jails and the patients are treated like inmates."

A father answered, "Have you visited a modern state home for mentally defective children? I think mentally defective people can live in as much dignity there as they can anyplace—more than in many homes. This idea that the staff of a state home has no respect for the individual patient was true at one time. Let's remember, though, that individuals got little respect anyplace. Industry's a good example. Not too long ago men worked under very poor conditions with long hours, poor pay, no safety regulations, no pensions—even children worked in factories and mines. Workers were often treated like slaves or animals. Things have changed. Society is concerned about the individual's working conditions and his rights must be respected by industry. Changes have taken place in state homes, too. Where I visited, the buildings and the patients were clean, the food was good. There was a school for the ones who could go to school. The ones who could work had jobs around the place. The staff was well trained and there were no bars on the windows. I think we need similar homes for cerebral palsied children who'll never be able to take care of themselves."

Obviously the members of this group of parents were worried

about the question—"What of the future?" Their children were all so severely involved that the parents recognized that independence and self care were out of the question. The following criteria which they set up seem to offer a sound basis for developing or selecting a future care program for children who cannot become sufficiently independent to take care of themselves:

1. Provision for adequate care.

Needs vary with the individual, so adequacy must be defined in terms of the needs of each handicapped person. Basic for all children would be good health care, good food, and an appropriate recreation program. For those who need speech, physical, or occupational therapy, these should be provided just as an educational program should be provided for those who can profit from instruction. While it would be wrong to deny these services to anyone needing them it is just as wrong for a parent to insist that a program be provided for children who don't need or can't profit from them.

2. An opportunity to live in dignity.

This idea was well expressed in a father's comment, "My boy will probably never be looked up to but I don't want him to be looked down on, either." Handicapped persons, regardless of the severity of their disability are individuals and an adequate future care program must so regard them. The concept of the dignity of man means basically that we respect him as an individual who has certain needs to be met, rights which are not to be violated, and privileges to be enjoyed. This is all parents want for their handicapped children. Parents recognize that handicapped children may be restricted in the extent to which they can exercise their rights and limited in the extent to which they can enjoy their privileges. They rightfully feel, however, that the degree of restriction and limitation is to be determined by the child's disability and not by the attitude of those caring for him.

3. *Guaranteed continuity of care.*

During a discussion of this point with a father and mother who were in disagreement about a care program for their child, the father said, "Look, we selected a family burial plot in a cemetery because it guaranteed to provide perpetual care. How can we ask less for a handicapped child while he's living?"

His wife replied, "Your illustration is certainly shocking but I'll have to admit that you've got a good point."

The problem of providing continuity of care is probably the greatest source of anxiety in thinking about the future. Parents want to know that nothing will disturb their handicapped child's security as long as he lives. Since he cannot provide security for himself they feel an urgent obligation to arrange it for him. Their attempts often end in frustration because adequate facilities are not available.

4. *Cost not to exceed parent's ability to pay.*

The cost of providing for a severely disabled person an adequate program in an environment where he can live in dignity with continuity of care assured is beyond the income of many parents. A reasonable and defensible point of view holds that this financial obligation is the responsibility of society as a whole rather than the sole obligation of the parent who by mischance has a handicapped child.

A Long-Term Plan Reduces Concern

Evaluated against these criteria many parents of mentally sub-normal and severely involved cerebral palsied children have found their plans wanting. Planning to keep the child at home always leaves unanswered for parents the question— What will happen after we're gone?" Plans to have a brother or sister take over after the parents are gone offer no greater guarantee of continuity of care and provide no assurance that the handicapped person can live in dignity. In their hearts parents know these things even though they may never have given voice to them. Herein lies a major source of worry which constantly nags the parents of severely handicapped children. Most of the members of this group felt that all their criteria could be met best by a residential type program operated with state financial support and under the supervision of an appropriate department of the state government. As public institutions, continuity of care could be maintained and the cost could be shared by all taxpayers. Supervision could be arranged which would establish and maintain a high quality program designed to provide adequate care and opportunities to live in dignity.

Many parents of children with intellectual impairments so severe as to preclude development of independence have found relief from their worry about the future by arranging for their children to live in state operated homes. Typical of the feelings of many parents were those expressed by a middle-aged couple, the parents of two children. Their 24-year-old son had completed college, was married, and had two children. Their 17-year-old son, Edgar, was mentally defective and it was obvious to the parents that he would never be able to take care of himself. His future was constantly on the minds of both parents. The father first brought Edgar to see me at the insistence of neighbors who felt that if only Edgar could learn to talk better he would not be so retarded. Our examination confirmed the father's belief that Edgar's speech was as good as could be expected of one with his mental ability. As usual, I asked the father what he was concerned about most.

Obviously eager for the chance to talk to someone he replied without a moment's hesitation, "The future!" He went on, "It's got so that I'm afraid to cross the street anymore for fear I might be hit by a car before I reach the other side. If I get a headache, I'm sure I'm having a stroke. If I get a pain in my chest, I'm sure it's a heart attack. All the time I keep worrying about how would Millie take care of Edgar without me. I used to think that Bob would take care of him but he's not around here anymore and besides he has a family and needs to lead a life of his own." Almost without pausing he continued, glad for the opportunity to speak the thoughts which he had kept bottled-up within him for so long, "Millie just can't manage him alone! He's too much for her and he gets her down. She's tied down with him all the time except for the short time each day when he's in a special kind of school and he won't be able to go there much longer. You can't trust him to be alone at home for any length of time. He can't go anyplace alone. She has to devote practically all her time—you might as well say all her life to him. Even when I'm around to help, he's still too much for her. I just don't know what we can do . . . ."

He paused and I asked him, "What are some of the things you've thought about doing?"

"Everything," he answered. "And I mean everything. Of course I'd never do it, but the idea has even crossed my mind that maybe it would be best if I found a way to end the lives of all three of us." He paused again and added guiltily, "That sounds terrible doesn't it? But sometimes it seems to be the only way out."

Again he paused uneasily and I remarked, "Many parents have mentioned considering this as one of the possible solutions to their problem. Like you, when they can't seem to think of anything else to do, the thought of just ending it all crosses their minds. What are some of the other things you've considered for Edgar?"

"Like I mentioned, we'd thought of having him live with Bob but that wouldn't be fair to Bob's wife or their children—for lots of reasons, that's out. Young couples have enough problems of their own without taking on someone else's."

"Have you ever considered arranging for Edgar to live in a home for retarded people?" I asked.

"Several years ago we investigated a special school where mentally retarded children could live but the charge for a year was more than I make and besides I don't think his mother would let him go anyway."

I said to him, "You know there are hundreds of parents in this state with the same kind of problem you have. To help them the state operates several large homes for mentally retarded children such as Edgar. Because they are tax supported you don't have to worry about expense. Have you ever considered arranging for Edgar to live in one of these homes?"

"I have thought about it," he replied. "But it's Millie. She wouldn't let him go and I wouldn't want to urge her to. She has a tough time with Edgar but she's made it her life. What I'm worried about is that if anything happens to me she'll eventually have to let him go somewhere else to live, but I won't be here to help her make arrangements. Is there any way we could make all the arrangements for Edgar to live in a state home but still keep him with us as long as we can manage? The arrangements would be sort of an insurance policy. I would know that everything had been done to make Edgar's future secure and I wouldn't be so afraid to cross the street."

This is the way Edgar's parents found some peace of mind. When I talked with his mother I found that she was just as worried about what would happen to Edgar if she became seriously ill or died. "His dad can't take care of him without me," was her comment. We encouraged them to visit the nearest state home and helped them make an application for Edgar's admission with the father and mother agreeing that they would keep him at home as long as they could manage. By keeping his application active they had what the father referred to as an "insurance policy."

Many parents of even young severely retarded children have decided to take out this kind of "insurance." The father of three young children told us that when it was discovered that his youngest child was mentally defective the doctor advised him to put the child in an institution. He said he was hurt and angered by this advice and made up his mind that Margie would stay with him as long as she lived. When a buddy was killed in a car crash he thought to himself, "My God, what if that had been me?" He said this made him realize what a problem his attitude could create for his wife. Knowing how he felt about placing Margie in an institution, his wife probably could not bring herself to do it if he died yet he asked, "What else could she do?" He realized his wife would have to get some kind of a job as soon as the children were in school but Margie wouldn't be going to school. He said he went to visit a state home and found it wasn't at all like he thought it would be. "It sounded so cold and prison-like when the doctor called it an institution," he said. He talked things over with his wife and they decided to make an application for Margie's admission. Together they agreed to keep Margie at home as long as they could but that if anything happened to either one of them the survivor would feel free to have Margie live in a state home if necessary. "This decision," he said, "took a big load off our minds."

Not all parents want to think of an application to a state home as an "insurance policy" to be cashed in at some future date. For various reasons, some parents decide to arrange for their mentally retarded child to enter a state program while he is quite young. A young professional man told me that their hyperactive mentally retarded son kept their home in a constant uproar. Night after night he returned from work to find his home like bedlam. They had been able to get no help in quieting the boy down. The other children were always worked up and his wife was too exhausted for any kind of family life. He said, "We've read a couple of books about the wonderful things a retarded child can do for a family like enriching the spiritual life and drawing the members of the family closer together. We've tried but that's not what's happening in our family. We're being torn apart!" He wanted help in arranging for their son to live in a state home as soon as possible.

The mother of an 18-year-old severely mentally retarded girl told me that she and her husband had decided to keep Ella with them as long as they lived but now felt they had made a wrong decision. The mother and father were college graduates and both held advanced degrees. Their other children, a daughter of about 17 and twin boys of 15, were honor students with talent in music and busy with many activities. The mother said that when Ella was young she fit right in with the rest of the family but, as they all grew older, Ella began to feel more and more out of place. This was not because the other members of the family deliberately pushed her aside, for they all loved her and were kind and thoughtful with her. Rather, it was because, as the children grew older, the social life had grown more complex. Not only were the other children involved in more activities, but guests of the parents included them in conversations and asked them to play the piano. The other children read books, attended lectures, watched TV programs, and kept up a constant chatter about all they were learning and enjoying. Since most of this was far beyond Ella's ability to understand there seemed to be no way to avoid Ella's frequent withdrawals to the sidelines. When her sister began driving the family car Ella cried. She wasn't allowed to drive, but she was "just as big." When a boy called with a corsage to take her sister to the high school prom, Ella wanted to know when a boy would take her to a dance. When Ella cried about it her mother said, "I thought my heart would break." In talking with parents of another adolescent mentally retarded child they learned he was so happy at the state home that he couldn't wait to return after a home visit. After hearing this, Ella's parents felt that had she gone to live at a home while young, she would have grown up with children of her own ability and interests and would not have been overwhelmed daily by the complexities of their family life and the achievements of her brothers and sisters. "I'm afraid we were motivated more by our own feelings than by an informed concern about Ella's future adjustment," her mother concluded.

———————

So it appears that the decision to keep a severely mentally retarded child at home has problems for some families beyond the question of who will care for the child after the parents are gone. From discussions with many parents about this problem it appears that the more complex the home environment, the more difficult it is for severely handicapped children to adjust. While they are young, these adjustment problems often go unnoticed by parents but in later years they can become of such major importance as to create inescapable difficulties regardless of the love and understanding given by the rest of the family.

On the other hand, parental peace of mind does not always result from early arrangements to have a child live in a state home as illustrated by the report of a mother who told me that for years she had been plagued by the question—"What would Louis be like today if I had kept him home?" They had followed their doctor's advice about early placement but now, 15 years later, weren't sure they had done the right thing. She said, "Maybe if we'd kept him with us and helped teach him he could have learned more."

I asked her, "Does Louis like it at the home?"

She replied, "Oh, yes, it isn't that he doesn't like it. It's more that we didn't even get to know him. We should have kept him with us at least until we could see for ourselves that he couldn't learn much. This way we have to take the word of other people for everything."

Important Decisions Cause Uncertainty

It seems that in complicated matters such as providing for the future of a severely handicapped child parents can't win complete freedom from worry. Whatever decision they make they may later question. In part, this is so because where our children are concerned we often have mixed feelings and ambiguous thoughts. We want them to grow up yet we don't want them to. A mother's tears have come to be as much a part of her daughter's wedding as her gleeful throwing of rice. From the mixture of sadness and pride as they debate the timing of his first haircut to the mixture of apprehension and pride as he leaves for college, parents can't tell whether to be happy or sad that their son is growing up. Seeing how difficult it is for parents to make decisions about their non-handicapped children and how often they feel unsure about the decisions they have made, we should not at all be surprised that parents have difficulty deciding if and when they should arrange for a severely handicapped child to live in a state home.

There are two important questions suggested by these comments of parents: Should parents make arrangements for their severely handicapped child to live in a state home? And, if so, when should the child enter the home? No one can answer these questions for any parent. Only by a careful analysis of their own situation can parents arrive at what, for them, are satisfactory answers. Some of the considerations which have helped parents think through these questions are:

1. Should we make arrangements for our severely handicapped child to live in a state home?

The basic consideration here is an objective estimate of the degree to which the child can learn to take care of himself. To live independently today one must be able to earn enough income to provide for his needs, be able to manage his money providently, be able to manage adequately the activities of daily living, and comport himself responsibly and in socially acceptable ways. The better a person can meet these requirements, the less supervision and help he requires. Many retarded and many physically handicapped children can function very satisfactorily in our society because they can meet the minimum requirements in each of these areas. For those who cannot be expected to obtain income sufficient for their needs, manage money providently, carry out the activities of daily living, and comport themselves responsibly and in socially acceptable ways, the question inevitably arises—"Who will take care of the child when the parents can no longer do so?" Many parents feel that the best available answer to this question is the state home.

2. When should a severely handicapped child begin to live in a state home?

The basic considerations here are the present and future feelings of the parents and of the handicapped child. If a child is placed in a home before the parents have had an opportunity to see for themselves that eventual independence is not possible because of intellectual or other limitations, they may later suffer agonizing doubts about the wisdom of their action. On the other hand, keeping a severely retarded child in a highly stimulating, complex social environment may lead him to be frustrated and unhappy. Another factor related to parents' feelings is seen in the tendency of some parents to make the severely handicapped child the focal point of their lives. This parental reaction has led some observers to feel that often the greatest tragedy is not the disability of the handicapped child but the loss to society which results from the restricted thinking and social withdrawal of his parents. In group discussions some parents of handicapped children have suggested that parents analyze the extent to which family life is dominated by the severely retarded or otherwise handicapped child and use this as a guide in determining when to have the child enter a state home.

Private Schools Perform Valuable Functions

At another meeting where the parents had conducted a discussion which led to the conclusion that a state sponsored home offered the best solution to the problem of caring for a child who would never be able to live independently, a mother asked, Does this mean that no one should consider sending his handicapped child to a private school?" Then she went on to say that she had investigated a number of privately operated schools for mentally retarded children. "Some of them have been in existence for a long time and there is every reason to believe that they will continue so I think continuity of care needn't worry anyone who wants to send his child to a private school and some schools will take children for long term care," she went on. "I was discussing this with a friend of ours who is a teacher and she said some of the best known doctors and other specialists are associated with private schools. I've heard that much research about things like the causes of mental retardation and about how to help these children is done at private schools. If these private schools are so good why do we say that a state operated program can best provide what we are looking for?"

A father replied, "I think the things you are saying about private schools are true. We checked into several of them when we were looking for a place for Freddie but we found that most of them wanted only those children who could make enough progress that eventually they could be discharged and we were looking for a place where Freddie could live when we could no longer take care of him."

Another mother joined in, "I think it all depends on what you're looking for. Sometimes we can't decide what kind of a program would be best for us and our child because we are not clear in our own minds about what we want the program to accomplish. If a special kind of teaching or treatment is what our child needs then we should send him to the kind of school or clinic where he can get it. If he doesn't need these special things but needs a place to live where people can do the things for him that he can't do for himself he can go to a different kind of home."

For some time the parents discussed the advantages and the disadvantages of state programs and private programs. Their conclusion seemed to be that there are many excellent private institutions, especially for the mentally retarded, but, as a rule, these are too costly for the average parent to consider even for short periods of training. A father expressed what most of the parents regarded as a practical point of view about private schools for mentally retarded children. "I know that many of them have excellent educational and treatment programs and some of them accept children for long term care," he said. "If Ben needed special help and I thought he could get it best at a private school, I'd go in debt to send him there. I'd mortgage my house and go without things. I'd want to be pretty sure, though, that they could do more for him than a state school could before I'd deny my wife and the other children things just to send Ben to a private school. From all I've learned about him though, he needs care and supervision, not treatment. Not many people have enough money to support a child in a private home for the rest of his life. I think it's wrong for parents to think they should give up all they have or ever hope to have just to keep a handicapped child in a private home. It's all right for people who have the money and don't have to weigh the cost of one thing against the cost of another thing. We shouldn't make the mistake of thinking that just because a school costs a lot it can make our child normal. I think private schools have an important place in a country like ours but for most of us government supported homes and schools will offer the best solution to our problem of providing care for a child who can't learn to care for himself."

While there are many good residential facilities for children with severe mental retardation, this is not true for children of unimpaired intellectual development who have severe physical disabilities. The parents of an adolescent girl who is severely disabled by cerebral palsy recently asked me to meet with a small group of parents to discuss the possibility of developing a residential facility for cerebral palsied adolescents of good mental ability. They organized the group and opened the discussion by saying, "Of course, we all want to keep our children with us as long as we can, but we must look ahead to the time when we won't be able to take care of them."

The father of a completely dependent adolescent boy said, "Let's be honest with ourselves and with each other right from the beginning. Sure, we can continue to take care of Butch for a long time, but it means that we will never have a chance to do the things other families do. I hope my wife and I can have a few years of freedom before we're too old. We've never been able to go anyplace or do anything together since Butch was a baby. I'm in favor of having a home where we can send our children to live whenever we want to."

No one disputed this idea and the members of the group went on to discuss what they wanted for their children. Their comments boiled down to an expression of the same criteria earlier expressed by the parents of retarded children. This group talked in terms of organizing 10 or 12 parents to finance the building and operation of a small residential facility for their children. Other parents have talked about urging the state to develop facilities to meet this need, while still others have discussed developing such programs under the sponsorship of appropriate voluntary health agencies. All of these proposals are attempts to answer that persistent question—"What of the future?" For parents of handicapped adolescents, the worry induced by this natural concern has become sharp because the future is upon them and their handicapped child.

Children Also Express Concern

That the children as well as the parents feel the weight of this concern, is illustrated by the conference I had with a teenage cerebral palsied girl whose severe involvement of all extremities precluded independent living. She asked her mother to leave as soon as her mother had pushed her wheel chair into my office. When she said, "They electrocute prisoners at

Rockview, don't they?," naming a prison a few miles from my office, I thought she was making conversation and replied, "Yes, that is where the state courts send criminals who have been sentenced to execution."

This time I caught the seriousness in her voice when she asked, "Could you help me arrange to be executed there?"

After waiting a moment to see if she would add anything, I observed, "Sometimes it kinda seems that life just isn't worth living, huh?"

"Not just sometimes," she came back quickly, "all the time!"

She went on to explain that it had been bad enough to have her parents dress her, feed her, wash her, and take care of her in the bathroom while she still hoped and believed that someday she could do these things for herself. Now that she knew self care was unattainable for her, it was unbearable for her to realize that her parents would have to do all these personal things for her as long as she lived.

"Some things you expect to do for a baby but not for a grown woman," she commented bitterly. "Some things they have to do for me you don't even have to do for a baby."

She explained that she was now worse than an infant for, in addition to needing the complete care of a baby, she now required extra help during her menstrual periods. "I can feel my mother cringe when she has to take care of me and, of course, Dad can't help with these things. Why should they have to devote their whole lives to taking care of someone who is worse than a baby?"

As we talked through her problem she said, "If our society won't execute worthless people like me, why doesn't it provide places for us to live so our parents won't have to give up their lives for us?"

For the purposes of this book we can't get too involved in discussing the emotional problems of the handicapped adolescent. Suffice to say that while in part this girl's questioning of her worthwhileness was a natural reaction of adolescence, her parents must recognize that she has problems which will not be solved by maturation. In fact, maturation has only made them worse. Any answering of the question—"What of the future?"—must, therefore, take into account the concerns of the child as well as those of the parents.

Parents Worry That Their Children Might Be Hurt

So far we have talked about worry in terms of the concerns which parents of severely disabled children feel about the future. While parents of less severely handicapped children do not have to worry about providing future care for a dependent individual, they, too, have concerns which produce worry and anxiety. A common source of worry stems from parents' very natural desire to protect their children from hurt and pain. Even animal parents try to protect their young from harm and lick their wounds for them when they are injured. Robins instinctively fly protectively overhead while their young are learning to fly ready to attack anything that threatens to harm their brood. Parents behave similarly when, for example, an operation is advised to correct a disabling condition. Usually their worry is tempered by the realization that the operation is in the child's best interest and that physicians and nurses will do everything possible to make the child comfortable. Even so, professional workers have come to expect parental anxiety to be aroused whenever hospitalization is advised. At cleft-palate clinics, when plastic surgery is recommended for the child, some parents immediately ask such questions as, "Is it a serious operation? How long will he be in the hospital? Will he have much pain? Won't he be frightened?" These questions quickly come to the minds of other parents but go unasked because their personalities don't permit them to give verbal expression to their anxieties. Still other parents experience a general kind of anxiety and can't think of specific questions until they are driving home or perhaps until the next day. Whether they express it or not, most parents find an operation a cause for worry which cannot be completely dispelled by a full explanation of what to expect.

Parents frequently regard operations as potential sources of pain to their children. More than once we have found those who have neglected to give various home treatments to their cerebral palsied child because, as they said, "The exercises hurt him." While such concern is understandable, here is an illustration of how uncontrolled worry can actually interfere with a child's habilitation. Sometimes parents have postponed making arrangements for dental care or surgical treatment of their children because of their concern that their child might be hurt. They try to hide, even from themselves, the real reason for their postponments by finding other plausible reasons, but often worry about hurting the child is the basis for their procrastination. Many times we have seen parents fail to make or fail to keep appointments for the psychological evaluation of their child. Sometimes valid reasons make it impossible to keep an appointment but often these appointments are not kept because parents are too worried about the outcome of the examination.

Worries Are Manageable
Some ways parents have found helpful in managing their

worries are illustrated by these excerpts from a parent discussion session.

"Worry, worry, worry!" a young mother of a disabled child said to the group. "All I do is worry about Marty."

"What do you worry about all the time?" another mother asked.

"I don't know," Marty's mother answered. "I just worry all the time. I wish I could stop this worrying."

"You'll never stop worrying until you find out what you're worrying about. That's the first thing you have to do—find out what's bothering you and then do something about it," suggested another mother.

Another mother said, "Don't wish that you can stop worrying because you can't. It's natural to worry. As long as there is still something wrong with your child you're going to worry some about it. Everytime he goes for another examination or an operation, you'll worry."

These parents had identified four important steps in managing one's worry about a handicapped child. They might be restated and amplified as follows:

1. Recognize that to worry is a natural reaction.

Since prehistoric times man has reacted with worry and anxiety when his security or that of his family has been threatened. Threats to the security of young birds and animals elicit parental behavior suggestive of instinctive concern about the safety of their offspring. Parents of handicapped children very naturally worry about the welfare of their children and feel concerned about anything that will hurt the child, even if the hurt results from some essential procedure such as surgery, dental care, or physical therapy. With severely handicapped children the question of future security is extremely anxiety provoking. In addition to recognizing the natural origins of worry, parents need to recognize that uncontrolled worry can actually interfere with their providing needed treatment for their child and block the development of adequate plans for his future.

2. Learn to identify the cause of worry.

Vague, non-specific worries are hard to cope with. Insofar as possible, parents should try to put into words for themselves a statement of what they are worried about. The mere verbalizing of what one's worried about often results in some reduction of the anxiety connected with it. Concerns often seem large when their boundaries are only vaguely perceived. Putting the concern into words establishes the boundaries and the size often shrinks. Identification of the causes of one's worry will show some to be only short term worries while others might be of longer duration. Worry about a child's operation, for example, will disappear when he has recovered from the surgery. On the other hand, worry about the future care of a dependent child will last much longer. Identification of the causes of worry will help prevent the merging of one's worries, large and small, short and long term, into a large unmanageable lump.

3. Work to eliminate the cause of the worry.

Taking direction for action from this statement of what they are worried about, parents can often minimize their worries. If one is concerned that his child will be hurt by an operation, for example, he can assure himself by talking with the doctor that procedures will be followed which will make the child as comfortable as possible. Thus assured, the parents can then do a better job of preparing the child for the operation. Better preparation of the child will, in itself, help to relieve their worries. If a parent is worried about providing future care for a child who will always be dependent, he cannot expect this worry to be relieved until he has worked out an adequate provision for the child. Worry fades away when one can successfully remove its cause.

4. Recognize that all worry cannot be eliminated.

Some people worry more than others but all people seem to have their anxious moments, which is only another way of saying that they worry at times. As one cause of worry is eliminated another often takes its place. Some causes can never be completely eliminated so a certain amount of anxiety remains. In addition to sharing man's general reasons for worrying, having a handicapped child creates additional sources of worry for parents. Instead of trying to eliminate all worry, it is more effective for one to minimize his worries by identifying them, classifying them, and trying to solve as many of the worry-creating problems as possible. Some authorities even feel that a little worry or anxiety is a good thing because it motivates man to desire and work for change. Without it, these theorists contend, man would quickly lapse into a deteriorating complacency. No one can ever find happiness if his goal is the shedding of all his worries. Peace of mind does come though to those who learn how to manage their worries.

It will be noted that the words "worry" and "anxiety" have been used interchangeably throughout this discussion. This has been done to help parents see the phrase "anxious parents" in proper perspective. A mother once told me that at a clinic she overheard a professional worker remark that she and her husband seemed to be "immobilized by their anxiety." She went on to say, "We've been worried sick about it ever since. All we can find out about anxiety is that it's a psychological problem—something like a neurosis, whatever that is. We're so worried about it that we're afraid to do anything for fear we'll do the wrong thing."

The person using the phrase, "immobilized by anxiety," probably could not have given a better explanation of what she meant than this mother had just given. She meant only that these parents were so anxious, that is to say so worried, that they couldn't move in any direction because they were afraid that whatever they would do would be wrong. Unfortunately this overheard professional jargon created more worry for the parents because they did not realize that professionals naturally use the language of their specialties rather than the words of lay people when describing a common experience. Just as parents don't feel alarmed when they hear a doctor refer to their child's broken leg as a fractured tibia, they should not feel distressed to hear their worries referred to as anxieties. Instead of saying, "These parents seem to be immobilized by their anxiety," the professional worker might just as well have said, "These parents seem to be so worried that they don't know what to do." Parents recognize that at times they are so worried that they don't know what to do, but somehow this doesn't seem as terrifying as being "immobilized by one's anxiety."

Worry and anxiety, then, are natural, common reactions of men. Probably no man can ever completely rid himself of them. Nor is this desirable. A more desirable goal would be to eliminate those worries for which the causes can be removed and to minimize worries for which the cause is not removable.

VIII

Children Have
Two Parents

Late one afternoon several years ago a father met me at my hotel and drove me to his home where I was to evaluate his 14-year-old daughter and talk with him and his wife about a program for her. They had read in a local paper that I was to participate in a clinic in their town and, saying that they preferred private rather than clinic services, they wrote asking if I could visit them at home. On the dirve to his home he told me about all the things they had tried to do for their daughter and how anxious they were to give her the best of everything. He said that despite all the help she had received she was still not able to take care of herself even though she could walk and use her hands almost normally. She had never been to school but her mother had been teaching her at home. "We think," he remarked, "That she'd be o.k. if only she could talk."

When I asked him why he thought she couldn't talk or take care of herself he said they had been told that she had cerebral palsy.

At their home I met his wife and the daughter, their only child. Both were charmingly dressed; the mother obviously wanted their daughter, Barbara, to make the very best impression. My first observation was that Barbara could and did talk but that her speech was difficult to understand because she misarticulated so many of the speech sounds and the comments she made were more like those of a pre-school child rather than those one would expect of a 14-year-old girl. Noting that Barbara reacted appropriately to instructions spoken by the mother even though she could not see her mother's face, I felt that she was not handicapped by a hearing loss. Her mother reported that Barbara had never had any difficulty with chewing, sucking, or swallowing. I could find no evidence of incoordination in movements of the speech structures. The only sign of cerebral palsy was a very slight involvement of the right leg and arm. Her mother described Barbara as a "quiet child who doesn't give me any trouble." When her mother told me that she had taught Barbara to read and write "all by myself" I asked her to show me what they were studying. Barbara could print her name but only if she copied it or her mother spelled it for her. Her reading consisted of the recognition of a few words. All in all, her development was about like that of a 5-year-old.

When I asked whether Barbara had ever gone to school, her mother burst out angrily, "No, I've tried to send her several times, but each time a man who calls himself a psychologist gives her some tests and then says she isn't ready for school. I've talked to the teachers and the principal and members of the school board but no one wants to help Barbara. They just don't understand her."

"When you take Barbara to your doctor, does he make any suggestions?" I asked.

"I don't take Barbara to a doctor any more. Our family doctor told me he couldn't do anything for her, so after she had all her shots we never went back. If she gets sick I take care of her myself."

Her husband had excused himself earlier and gone outdoors so I asked, "What does your husband think about Barbara's difficulty?"

"He's just like everybody else," she retorted. "You'd think she wasn't his daughter the way he acts." With a note of finality she added, "We just don't talk about it anymore."

"I see. You can't agree about Barbara's problems so you don't discuss them any more," I said. "What has been your husband's point of view?"

"Well, he thinks everybody else is right and I am wrong. He said she wasn't ready for school because she has the mentality of a baby. How could he say such a thing about his own daughter? He gets angry with me because he thinks I spend too much time with Barbara and because I think she should go every place we go. We fought so much that now Barbara and I lead our own lives and he leads his."

It seemed obvious that Barbara's primary problem was her severe mental retardation. It was equally obvious that her mother was not yet able to accept this diagnosis. Realizing that in one short conference I could do little to help her understand

and accept Barbara's intellectual limitations, I merely tried to get her to rule out other possible causes of Barbara's speech problem.

To my question—"Do you think Barbara's hearing is all right?"—she responded, "Oh, yes! She hears everything." To my inquiry—"How about her tongue? Does it seem to work all right?"—she replied, "Her tongue is perfectly all right. Her only problem is that she's never been taught anything except what I teach her." I then made suggestions about teaching materials and techniques pointing out that pre-first grade materials would be most appropriate for Barbara. Since she had seemed so hostile to the school psychologist and her doctor I carefully avoided any suggestion that she talk with any other professional people. Instead, I suggested that she might get some helpful ideas by talking with other parents of children who had difficulty in learning to talk, read, and write.

As soon as the father and I entered the car to drive back to the hotel, he blurted out, "I'd divorce that woman in a minute, but I can't leave her with all the responsibility for Barbara. You know as well as I do that Barbara is feeble-minded but do you think anyone can make my wife see it? A number of years ago we used to take Barbara to the crippled children's clinic but my wife got mad at them when they suggested Barbara was retarded. The school people hate to see her come and our doctor told me that he can't do anything with her. She won't even let our minister talk with her. She won't let me say anything. You'd think Barbara had only one parent the way her mother has pushed me aside."

This family needed lots of help, but, as illustrated by the experience of the doctor, psychologist, and other professional workers, it is difficult to help anyone who strongly resists help. In this one brief contact with the family I didn't learn why the mother had to insist on the normality of her daughter. Perhaps through group discussions with other parents she could have developed greater insight into her feelings and an acceptance of her daughter's limitations. Unfortunately, group counseling was not available in their community. It seemed that nothing could be done to help them become a two-parent family.

The mother of a severely disabled 6-year-old boy used the same bitter phrase—"You'd think Eddie had only one parent"— in telling me about how she found it impossible to be a "nurse, physical therapist, cook, cleaning lady, purchasing agent, and affectionate wife." An attractive young mother of three children, she said she was at her wit's end trying to do everything.

"Bob complains that I never have time for him anymore. He says I never want to go anyplace and that I'm always too tired or too tense to make love. A couple of days ago he told my mother that he may as well not have a wife anymore. I was hurt but when I thought about it I could see that he was right. And then I thought about it some more and I'm gonna tell him one of these days I don't have a husband either. Bob never helps me with anything. He won't feed Eddie, take him to the bathroom, put on his braces, give him his exercises, or anything. For all his daddy ever does for him you'd think Eddie had only one parent."

When I talked with her husband he told me that he hardly had a wife anymore. He said, "I married her because I loved her and I still want to love her but she won't let me. She's always too busy with that kid. We were having a good time together until he took up all her time and energy. She thinks I ought to help more, but I'm tired when I come home and I want to rest instead of starting in to work again."

Marital Happiness Must Be Earned

Many parents of handicapped children have thought all their marital difficulties were traceable to their having a handicapped child. Undoubtedly having a handicapped child creates special strains on a marital relationship because of the extra demands on time, energy, family income, and the inevitable influences a handicapped child has on parental attitudes and feelings. However, one need only recall the old nursery rhyme to realize that the handicapped child is unlikely to be the sole source of his parents' marital problems:

Needles and pins, needles and pins,
When a man marries his trouble begins.

In all probability, the anonymous author of this couplet was a male, for under female authorship the second line would have read:

When a girl marries her trouble begins.

And so it has been down through the ages. Menander, who lived 300 years before Christ, wrote: "Marriage, if one will face the truth, is an evil, but a necessary evil." Some observers of the matrimonial scene have likened marriage to a bird cage with the birds on the outside trying to get in and the birds on the inside trying to get out. Many factors are at work in our society to increase the number trying to get out. Lawrence Bee, in *Marriage and Family Relations,* points out: "In the United States today there is one divorce granted for every three to four marriage licenses issued." From this observation and his estimate that between 20 and 45 percent of all divorce cases filed are dismissed, one gets the definite impression that there is much serious marital discord in the United States. How many more husbands and wives become estranged without filing for divorce because of religious or other reasons is anybody's guess. The suggestion that all married couples have some periods of estrangement is based on more than idle speculation. How can two personalities live forever in perfect harmony within the intimately close confines of marriage? Many, if not most, young people assume that their marriage license entitles them to marital happiness. It doesn't. As pointed out in the Declaration of Independence, man's right is only to the *pursuit* of happiness. Ibsen was aware of this when he wrote: "Marriage is a thing you've got to give your whole mind to." Certainly marital happiness is something a husband and wife must plan for and ever work toward achieving. Not many hold this point of view, so it is little wonder that marital discord is so rampant in this day.

Considered as a group, the parents of handicapped children would have the same problems of marital adjustment as all other husbands and wives. Even if they had no handicapped children all of them might expect to have some problems of adjustment. Having a handicapped child tends to make it more difficult for the husband and wife to work out adjustments to each other. When estrangements occur, parents will find the cause in themselves not in the handicapped child. That the causes of marital problems lie in the parents is suggested by Fosdick's statement: "It is not marriage that fails; it is people that fail. All that marriage does is show people up." Certainly having a handicapped child calls for stronger efforts on the part of both parents to adjust to this as well as the many other problems of married life.

Handicapped Children Affect Marriage Relationship

Many parents have talked about their marriage problems when we have been discussing the feelings of parents of handicapped children. I have no statistics and know of no formal research on this point, but it is my definite impression that most parents of severely handicapped children at some time or other have serious disagreements growing out of problems related to their handicapped children. While it is undoubtedly true that parents of non-handicapped children also have disagreements stemming from problems with their children, the natural emotionality and the complexity of the problems associated with having a handicapped child seem to provide a more fertile ground in which discord can grow. More than one set of parents has told me that they no longer sleep together because they are afraid they might have another handicapped child. Some have even been afraid to have any more children at all, saying that with the handicapped child they just couldn't take care of another child. Many a husband has said in effect, "I lost my wife to our handicapped child." Their complaint that their wives give all their time and energy to the care of the handicapped child, reserving none for normal family living, is often valid. Their wives' complaints that the husbands don't help enough with the care of the children is usually equally valid. Disagreements about planning for the future care of a severely handicapped child are common. Often parents do not initially see eye to eye about who should take care of the child in the event something happened to the parents. Husband and wife often vary widely in the objectivity of their assessment of their child's limitations and capabilities. One will indulge in wishful thinking while the other develops a more realistic appraisal. Unfortunately parents often try to handle these problems by trying to ignore them. Frequently parents have told me that any discussion of their handicapped child was taboo in their home. In talking with these families one often gets the impression that really, instead of driving his parents apart, the handicapped child is the major force in keeping them together. Fortunately, as Linton points out in *The Family: Its Function and Destiny:* "The ancient trinity of father, mother, and child has survived more vicissitudes than any other human relationship."

What can parents do to ease the natural marital frictions associated with parenthood of a handicapped child? The following remarks selected from a number of discussions with parents offer helpful suggestions:

"My wife and I seemed to be arguing with each other about something almost every day." This was the father of a 6-year-old cerebral palsied boy speaking. "It had got so we weren't very happy together anymore and I was mad because I felt my wife was cheating me out of a happy marriage. One night when I was playing cards with a bunch of guys, they got to kidding each other about fighting with their wives and I suddenly realized that marriage must be a series of ups and downs for everybody. I guess I had the romantic notion that a happy marriage is just a big long honeymoon. That's just a kid's notion. I grew up a little bit more while I listened to those guys talk. I quit feeling that I'd been cheated out of happiness. I realized that whenever two people both form opinions about things, some of the opinions are going to differ. We felt so mad every time we disagreed about something that we automatically started to fight about it. I think this was partly because we thought happy people don't disagree and we were mad because we were making each other unhappy. After that card party I learned how to laugh and kid with my wife about a lot of our disagreements. When we learned that you can disagree and still be happy together we actually quit arguing so much."

The parents of a mentally retarded girl told me that their whole attitude toward each other changed when their minister explained to them that a happy marriage is not one in which there are no disagreements but rather it is one in which the mates learn to disagree without being disagreeable.

"He told us that some unpleasantness was unavoidable in marital relationships but that the pleasantness should outweigh the unpleasantness," the mother said.

The father explained, "We think of having two piles. In one we stack up our unpleasant experiences with each other and in the second pile we stack our pleasant experiences together. Our job is to see that the second pile is always much higher than the first. This means that we both have to keep working at having a happy marriage."

"That's right," his wife added. "No one ever makes you happy—you really have to make yourself happy. Happiness is all within you."

The father of an 8-year-old boy who was severely handicapped by cerebral palsy and mental retardation said his relations with his wife took a definite turn for the better after he had to take over the house and children for a few days while she was sick. "I never really had any idea of what her day was like until I had to try to take her place," he said. "I started early in the morning and kept going until late at night without a minute's rest. I know it took me longer to do some things because I hadn't done them before, but I didn't even get to a lot of things she does either. When I was trying to get supper I thought about how much easier it would be if the kids weren't underfoot. This made me realize that I ought to entertain the kids when I get home from work so my wife can have a few minutes peace while she's getting supper. Now I give her a hand more with the kids and with things around the house. Her disposition's improved and we get along a lot better."

I know from personal experience how easy it is for a husband to come home from work, sink into a chair with the evening paper, and wait for his wife to call him to the table. I had been doing it for several years and while our children were infants my wife did not object. When our first child began to walk and talk she would climb eagerly on my lap and employ many techniques designed to direct my attention to her and away from the *Centre Daily Times.* After a few minutes I would gently put her on the floor saying, "I'll play with you after awhile, honey. Right now Daddy's tired and wants to sit and read the paper." How long this went on I don't know. One evening my wife came in and affectionately sat on my lap, putting her arms around me, and kissed me tenderly a few times. My ego began to expand in response to her comments that she was proud of me and especially of the way I helped so many people with their problems. She said she thought it was wonderful that I took such an interest in the feelings of parents and their handicapped children. I began to wonder if she had been talking that afternoon with a family from one of the clinics or perhaps, even a staff member. When she had built my feelings of worthwhileness to a high level she said, "I'm glad I have someone like you to talk to because I know of a little girl who can't wait for her father to come home and when he puts her off his lap so he can read the paper she goes into the kitchen half crying and interferes with her mother when she's trying to get dinner ready. The mother and little girl don't like it and they are beginning to feel quite hostile toward the father. Do you think you could help this family?"

At an evening discussion session several members of a group of mothers of cerebral palsied children were quite outspoken about their husband's failures to help around the house and their seeming disinterest in their handicapped child.

One mother criticized, "My husband uses his home as a place to eat, watch TV, and sleep. We used to go to a movie on Saturday night and for a ride on Sunday. Now he says we can watch movies on TV. He says it's too much trouble to get all the kids in the car for a ride on Sunday. So, I have to stay home all the time. I even had trouble getting him to watch the children so I could come to these meetings."

"I know what you mean," another mother joined in. "I wish these meetings would go on forever 'cause they give me a chance to get out at least once a week. John won't even go to the clinics with me, yet he keeps asking, 'How come it's taking so long for little John to learn to walk?' How can I explain anything to him? He doesn't know what the therapists are trying to do. He just doesn't understand anything about little John!"

"My biggest gripe is that my husband never sees what needs to be done. If I ask him to do something, he'll do it but he never offers to help or he never pitches right in. I get tired of asking him and asking him. You'd think that by now he'd have caught on that I need help. When you have a child like Marvin there's a lot of extra things to be done. I wouldn't expect him to take care of Marvin all the time but I need a break now and then. I don't know why he can't see that."

"Maybe one reason is because husbands are so soft hearted," suggested another mother. "One time my husband started to feed our boy his supper. I had everything chopped up because he can't chew. My husband gave Georgie a few bites but when Georgie started to gag and the food started to dribble out of the corners of him mouth big tears came into my husband's eyes and he got up and walked away. He's never fed Georgie since."

"I think husbands grieve twice," an older mother observed. "Once for their handicapped child and once for their wives. I'm used to taking care of Connie so it doesn't bother me so much anymore. Her dad still chokes up and gets all nervous when he has to dress her or feed her. It seems that these things remind him of how handicapped she is. I'm sure he gets out of doing things for her because it hurts him too much. And I know he grieves for me, too. I can tell by the way he acts that he feels sorry for me that I don't have any normal children."

At a meeting of a different group a mother started the others thinking with her observation that wives can do a lot to determine what attitudes their husbands develop.

"One day my sister dropped in just about time for my husband to come from work," she said to the group. "When she saw me, she said, 'Whatcha trying to do, Lucille, scare Harve away?' I told her that I was tired and had been so busy that I didn't have time to clean myself up. My sister told me she'd read an article about how important it was for a wife to keep an interest in her appearance. She said 'How are you gonna keep Harve interested in you if you're not interested in yourself?' She made me realize that I had quit making any effort to be interesting or attractive to Harve. When I began to fix myself up a little I began to feel more cheerful myself. I'm not saying that this is the solution to all family problems but I think it changes the home atmosphere a lot."

Another mother picked up the idea. "That's right. Attitudes are learned unconsciously. A husband doesn't consciously say to himself, 'I'm not interested in my wife or family anymore.' When he comes home from work tired and finds his wife looking bedraggled and ready with a lot of problems for him he feels even more tired. Subconsciously he thinks, 'Aw, the hell with everything.' When this happens night after night it soon becomes his whole attitude. I think we ought to look as nice as we can and make an effort to be pleasant when our husbands come home. It's not fair to hit the guy between the eyes with all his home problems as soon as he steps into the house."

From these remarks we can draw some suggestions about how husbands and wives might learn to live more happily together and how they can work together to provide for their handicapped child a two-parent family:

1. Recognize that some disagreements are inevitable in marriage.

For two people to live together day after day without ever disagreeing is impossible. Husbands and wives are bound to face problems about which each has personal feelings and ideas. Since few people have learned to divorce their personalities from their ideas, any challenge of their opinion is interpreted in personal terms and clashes of personalities result. Outside the home, many forces operate to cause people to inhibit their emotional reactions when disagreements occur. With one's mate one feels freer to "blow his top" when an opinion is challenged or a point of view is ignored. Husbands and wives need to recognize disagreement for what it is—two personalities expressing different points of view. They need also to recognize their emotional reactions for what they are—a defensive response to the challenging of one's ideas. These two concepts can help keep disagreements intellectual in tone and prevent them from pyramiding into emotionally toned family discord.

2. Recognize that the pursuit of marital happiness is a life-long obligation.

Happiness is a state of mind and as such is elusive and transient. Its presence often tells more about its possessor than about the people or events in his life. While we speak of the "pursuit" of happiness, it never can be caught. Rather, happiness must be earned, just as in education one pursues his studies but earns a degree. To achieve happiness in marriage one must create the atmosphere and do the things which produce in him the state of mind he calls happiness. Only by conscious and continual effort can an atmosphere conducive to the achievement of happiness be maintained. This effort must include casting one's own concept of happiness in realistic terms and trying to create the atmosphere which helps his mate achieve happiness. The only way man can hold on to happiness is through his awareness of the conditions which make others happy and his constant efforts to create these conditions. When husband and wife both subscribe to this point of view and act on it, marital discord will be minimal.

3. Share the work.

Caring effectively for children requires more than providing food, shelter, and clothing. The less obvious, but equally important, psychological needs of children must also be met. Add to this the prolonged physical care which severely handicapped children need, and the amount of time and energy required is substantial. Husbands work all day and are tired when evening comes. Wives work all day, too, and they are also tired when evening comes. Yet there remains work to be done. Sharing of the evening and weekend care of a handicapped child would seem to be called for by one's sense of fairness. Not only will a father's helping care for the child make his wife's workload lighter, but there is no better way for a father to develop a first-hand knowledge of his child's capabilities and limitations than by routine caring for him. The child also benefits psychologically from seeing that both his parents care for him. All these factors make sharing the work an important feature of being a two-parent family and an important step toward creating the atmosphere out of which marital happiness develops.

4. Learn how to talk together about your problems.

A key part of this suggestion is the idea of learning *how* to talk together. As was pointed out earlier, many people permit their feelings to get out of hand and interfere with a rational consideration of a problem. When a husband and wife learn to keep their tempers in check and learn not to react emotionally to their mate's outbursts of temper they are better able to find solutions to their problems. Also important is learning to talk spirally rather than circularly. Many people talk around in circles, that is to say, they have their minds made up and regardless of how much they talk around a subject they come back to their preconceived point of view. No revision of their thinking occurs. No growth of an idea takes place. In a spiralling discussion there are interactions of points of view with each participant modifying his ideas as a result of what is said by others. In this way the consideration of a problem does not circle around and around in restatements of stubbornly held points of view as if the discussants were in a rut. Instead the discussion moves progressively toward the center or core of the problem under consideration just as the line of a spiral gradually approaches a central point. When one talks in circles he need pay no attention to what anyone else says because he intends to return to his starting point. In a spiralling discussion a husband or wife must not only pay attention to what the other says but consciously try to adjust his point of view in terms of what the other contributes to an understanding of the problem. In addition to the usual problems which confront a husband and wife, having a handicapped child produces special problems. Through effective discussion parents can work together to solve these problems.

Suspicion Weakens Marriage Ties

Another cause of tension between the parents of a handicapped child is seen in the following remarks of a young mother. I had asked her what she thought was the cause of her child's cleft palate.

"Well, I'm sure of one thing," she said. "There was nothing wrong in my family. But you know, I didn't know my husband very long before we got married and I still haven't met all his relatives. I strongly suspect that there's a skeleton in his closet somewhere."

A husband confided to me, "I've never said anything to my wife about this because I wouldn't want to hurt her feelings, but she has some mighty queer relatives. They get along all right but they do some awfully crazy things. I have a feeling that there's an odd strain of some kind running through that family and all the bad features of it are concentrated in Billy. That's why he's so dull."

The mother of a cerebral palsied girl said, "Oh, he denies it all right, but I'm as sure as anything that my husband has brought this on us. I never did anything, so who else could it be? There has to be a reason for it. All men do things they won't admit and Ed's no different. I wish he'd come right out and admit it so I could get it off my mind."

This suspicion that one's mate is in some way responsible for the family's having a handicapped child has its origin in two common parental reactions. First, there is the strong impulse to explain why it had to happen which has been discussed earlier. Second, there is the natural human desire to protect one's own personality. Just as our bodies rush white corpuscles to the site of a wound to ward off invading bacteria, our personalities throw up various kinds of defenses to prevent our feelings from being hurt. One of these defenses is suspicion. If a parent can suspect that his mate is in some way responsible for their having a handicapped child, he or she is absolved of any blame. While only a few parents have come right out and discussed their suspicions with me, I get the impression that suspicions at least flit across the minds of a great many parents of handicapped children. Even unspoken suspicion can gnaw away at the foundations of a marriage. As one parent put it: "Suspicion destroys faith." Faith in each other is one of the keystones of a two-parent family. Earlier we talked about "chariot" and "bow and arrow" explanations of the sun in contrast with modern scientific explanations. Explaining the birth of a handicapped child in terms of some suspected action of a mate or some skeleton in the mate's family closet is akin to pre-scientific explanations of the sun. As parents acquire scientific information about the nature of their child's handicap and its causes, they will agree with Samuel Johnson who said: "Suspicion is very often a useless pain."

That children have two parents when they start life is a biological fact which escapes no one. In our culture, however, there are many forces at work to pull these parents apart. These forces operate on the parents of handicapped children plus additional forces related to the problems of having a disabled child. Too frequently, even when his parents continue to live together, the handicapped child has in effect only a one-parent family. Parental understanding of the forces which lead to this unhappy family situation can help the handicapped child enjoy the advantages of having two parents. It can help the parents enjoy their lives more fully, also.

IX

Faith of Their Fathers

While consulting in a school system a number of years ago my attention was called to a fourth-grade girl who spoke very defectively. She was described by her teacher as being very shy and withdrawn and as not working up to her capacity. My examination revealed that she had a cleft palate for which she had never received any attention. On checking with the school nurse about referring the child to a group of specialists, I learned that, for religious reasons, the child's parents refused to have anything done for her. The parents rejected every suggestion that a reconstruction of their child's palate was essential to her health, the development of good speech, and to her school and social adjustment. Feeling that the parents must not understand how handicapping the cleft palate was for Bonnie, I decided to visit them in their home late that afternoon. Bonnie's mother readily admitted me when I told her who I was and, as she invited me to sit in the living room, she explained that her husband was working late. I immediately noted that the walls were adorned with pictures of religious significance. On a table there was an open and obviously well-thumbed Bible. Several religious tracts were lying on the sofa and there were others on the table by the Bible. I tried to talk with Bonnie's mother about Bonnie's cleft palate and what could be done for it. I explained how important it was for Bonnie to have her palate repaired. Bonnie's mother listened politely and finally said,

"If God had wanted Bonnie to be different, He would have made her different Himself. We can't go against God's will." Sensing that further discussion would not alter her opinion, I allowed her to direct our conversation into other channels for a few minutes. As I prepared to depart, I said I would like to talk with her husband and asked if he would be free to come to my hotel that evening.

"Oh, no!" she said, "He'd never go in there. There's a bar in that hotel."

I made arrangements to return to the home later that evening to talk with Bonnie's father who, as I anticipated, turned out to hold the same beliefs her mother had expressed earlier. When I asked him what made him feel that God did not want anything done about Bonnie's cleft palate, he said she was born that way so that must be the way God wanted her to be. I asked him what kind of clothes he had on when he was born and his reply—"None"—led me to inquire, "Why do you not live in the nude since that's the way you were born? According to your reasoning, wouldn't God have clothed you in some manner if He wanted you to wear clothing?"

"No," he said. "That's different." And he launched into a long explanation about God's will which I couldn't follow. When he finished he assumed that he had adequately explained why it was all right for him to wear clothes though born nude but it would not be all right to have his daughter's cleft palate repaired because she was born with her palate open. Somewhere in his discussion I guess I missed the point but there was nothing to be gained by pursuing it further.

When I returned to talking about how difficult it would be for Bonnie to get along in life unless she had her palate repaired and how I could make all the necessary arrangements to have a group of specialists see Bonnie and talk with him, he told me in no uncertain terms that I was being meddlesome. He wanted no such help and assured me that he could bring up Bonnie in "God's way" and that this was his right.

Parents Are Entitled to Freedom of Worship

Freedom to worship as we wish is cherished by our people. This freedom is guaranteed by the first amendment to the Constitution of the United States which says: "Congress shall make no law respecting an establishment of religion, or prohibiting the free exercise thereof . . . ." In view of such a strong tradition of religious freedom one can readily understand why Bonnie's father resented any action which seemed to him an infringement on his religious beliefs. His right to believe as he will is undeniable—so long as his beliefs don't give him license to violate the rights of others. Obviously our society would not today permit a type of religious worship which included sacrificial offerings of animal or human life. Legal action has been taken to outlaw polygamy and polygamists have been punished even though they argued that their church instructed them to engage in plural marriages. What of Bonnie's rights? Who will fight to defend her against the life of unhappiness and lowered achievement decreed by her father's religious beliefs? In ancient Sparta malformed infants were exposed to die in the city's outskirts. We are repelled by the thought, but might this not be more humanitarian than to sentence a child to a very limited kind of life when, but for the "religious" beliefs of her parents, she could be helped to lead a happy, useful life. Only by closing their eyes to the injustice they are doing their handicapped child can these parents find peace of mind in their faith.

A somewhat different point of view, but one which also interfered with the development of an adequate program for a handicapped child, was held by the mother of a severely retarded boy. She contended that man, specifically the doctors, nurses, and therapists, was responsible for her son's condition but God, working through her, would make her son into a normal person. She brought her son, who was then 21, to our clinic hoping that we would accept him for speech therapy. In telling us about his problem she said that the doctors did not expect him to live when he was born but "with God's help" she had nursed him "back to strength." When he was a year old a doctor had told her that Paul would not learn to walk or talk and that he would never be able to go to school. He advised institutionalization. Again with God's help, she had exercised his legs and feet and by his fifth birthday, Paul was walking. In telling me about these experiences, Paul's mother said, "Twice, with God's help, I outsmarted the doctors. They said he wouldn't live and God and I nursed him back to strength. They said he wouldn't walk and God and I taught him to walk. With God's help, I'll teach him to read and write and everything else." Why she felt she needed our help to teach him to talk, we never found out.

Our examination showed that Paul's mental ability was comparable to that of the average 5 to 6-year old. His hearing was normal and we found no significant problem in coordination beyond a slight clumsiness. Our findings and his history pointed to mental retardation. At his age speech therapy was not indicated. Despite our best efforts to explain that Paul's retarded mental development was the main reason he did not walk until he was 5 years of age and that he would have walked at that age even if she hadn't exercised his legs, his mother insisted that it was God, working through her, who had made Paul walk. When we explained that we did not think speech therapy would be helpful, she said she had expected us to say that because we did not understand "Paul's relationship with God." If only we could understand how God worked we could be of more assistance to people like Paul, she suggested. In a polite but intense way she contended that all professional workers needed more faith in God and not until they found this faith would they be fully prepared to help handicapped persons. "By themselves," she said, "doctors, psychologists, and therapists can't do anything for handicapped children. It's only when God works through them that they accomplish any good."

Many people, including some "doctors, psychologists, and therapists" might share the belief that God works through man to achieve His will on earth. It is not our purpose here to discuss the theological soundness of this concept. Rather, we want to point out how the blind faith of Paul's mother interfered with the proper management of his problem. Because I was interested in getting her point of view, I encouraged Paul's mother to talk at length about her feelings toward professional people. From her remarks it seemed clear that her faith provided an ever-ready and powerful defense against what she did not want to hear. She dismissed the diagnoses and recommendations of the many professional workers who had evaluated Paul with the statement that they were "faithless" people. Why did she regard them as faithless? Because they said Paul was mentally retarded and that nothing could be done to push his development beyond an elementary level. Armed with the belief that anyone with sufficient faith in God could help Paul, she fought off all unfavorable professional opinions. She had hardly listened when I had tried to interpret the results of our evaluation of Paul. As soon as she surmised that we were not going to accept him for treatment she closed her mind, strong in her belief that "faithless" people speak only untruths. She seemed to miss entirely the point that not only did we feel he could not be helped by speech therapy but that he lacked the social competency necessary for living away from home without close supervision. When we asked her what other examiners had reported about Paul she seemed to have little specific information yet we had received copies of reports indicating that he had been carefully evaluated on several occasions. It appeared that she had learned little about Paul's problem from any of the professional people who had tried to counsel her; hence, it could hardly be expected that she would have followed any of their recommendations.

Later I had an opportunity to talk with parents of other handicapped children from the area where Paul lived. His mother's influence was evident. She was an ardent crusader for the point of view that God, working through the parents, could do more for handicapped children than any professionally

trained specialists could do. One father became extremely annoyed with his wife when she began to express some of the
points of view which Paul's mother had expounded. "That woman," he said, referring to Paul's mother, "is getting you all
mixed up. We used to be able to talk together about Wendy
but now you won't listen to anyone anymore. You'd think she
was one of the disciples the way you fall for her preaching."
It was with real concern for the welfare of handicapped children and the peace of mind of their parents that I learned a
year or so later that Paul's mother had been elected to a key
office in a newly-formed program for handicapped children.

Problems Can and Do Exist

The Reverend John D. Lee in a little booklet titled *Why Did
This Have to Happen to Me* suggests a different faith when he
writes:

> *A Christian looks at suffering in this manner:
> Here, he says to himself, is a condition. It is
> present. It is real. Since it exists, then God has
> permitted it to exist. And since God has permitted
> it, He has a purpose in it. My task is to find out,
> if I can, what purpose God has in mind for me,
> what final goal He hopes to bring about. Ob-
> viously, what He wants me to become is still
> possible for me with this pain, this disease, this
> suffering. What does God want me to do with it,
> so that, through it I can become the kind of per-
> son God wants me to become?*
>
> *To do this is to take the pain and suffering and
> put it into its proper place. No longer can one*

> *sit and bemoan one's lot, as though it were much,*
> *much worse than that of anyone else. One must,*
> *to bring one's ailment, whatever it may be, out*
> *in the open, look at it steadily and then, with the*
> *best that we can understand of what God wants*
> *us to do with it, proceed to that end.*

Dr. Lee goes on to suggest that the question—"Why did this have to happen to me?"—is quite presumptuous. "Well, why not?" he asks. "Are we fate's favorites, out of all mankind?"

I once heard a husband try to quiet his tearful wife with the comment, "Honey, you just tear yourself apart with that question—'Why did this have to happen to us?' Who are we that it shouldn't happen to us? These things happen to many people. Everyone has problems of some kind. That's the way life is. Some seem bigger than others but who can tell? I don't think we would trade our problems with very many people. What we have to do is face our problems squarely and still make the most of our lives. Maybe we can even live better lives because of our problems with Robbie." While this father did not specifically talk in terms of what God had in mind, his point of view is in many ways similar to that expressed by Dr. Lee. There is the recognition that, as Dr. Lee has put it: ". . . suffering of one kind or another is the common lot. No one gets through this world without a certain amount of it, less for some, more for others." There is also the recognition that problems can and do exist. They are real—not illusions. They must be faced squarely and managed in such a way that they do not prevent a family from learning to live a happy, useful life.

Some parents have bitterly denounced God because, as they say, "He has let our child be handicapped." Others have felt, too, that the presence of handicapped children in the world casts doubts on the existence of a "just God," but instead of being bitter they are sad. This point of view was expressed in a discussion group by the mother of a child who was severely disabled by cerebral palsy.

"I want to believe in God," she told the group and added in a softer voice almost as if saying it to herself, "And I need to." Then louder, she went on, "But how can I? If there is a God, why did He let our child be so helpless? Why does He make us suffer so? Look at all the really sinful people who never have anything happen to them. If there is a God why does He pass them over and then afflict a newborn baby that's so sweet and pure?"

The mother of a teen-age boy who had become paralyzed through an accident in which an automobile had collided with his bicycle answered, "I used to wonder about that, too. My boy was always a good boy. He went to Sunday school and didn't smoke or swear yet he is the one who was hurt. I used to wonder why God hadn't hurt some of those 'juvenile delinquents' in our neighborhood instead. Then I read in the paper one night how a bunch of crazy kids were driving home from a party and the car went out of control and rolled over a hill. One of the boys—a real gangster type—was killed and several of the others were hurt pretty bad. I got to thinking that all kinds of people are injured by automobiles. It all depends on who is there when something goes wrong. If a car goes out of control the people in it will get hurt whether they are good people or bad people. I don't think being pure or sinful has anything to do with it. Good people can be just as careless as bad people and God isn't going to protect them if they're careless."

Dr. Robert R. Youngs, in an article written for the Laymen's Movement for a Christian World, had this to say:

> . . . *the Bible reminds us that good people sometimes suffer because God through nature can be no respecter of persons. ("He maketh His sun to rise on the evil and on the good, and sendeth rain on the just and on the unjust.") This is a world of law and order, where all people are subject to cause and effect regardless of their virtue or lack of it. Good people are just as susceptible as bad people when they are exposed to contagious diseases. They strike the ground just as forcibly when they slip and fall. The world would be an unscientific and unpredictable place in which to live if it were not this way.*

Nature Is Lawful and Orderly

Dr. Young's comments about our living in a world of law and order, where all people are subject to cause and effect, remind us of the mother's remarks reported in our discussion of "Who's to Blame?" She said, it will be recalled, "People a long time ago used to blame God for everything—famines, plagues, floods . . . . Now we don't have to blame God for famines, plagues, and floods because we know more about them . . . ." The point here is that there are certain laws which govern natural phenomena and produce order in our world. Throughout history man has been busily trying to identify these laws and trying to understand the order of nature. Much of his effort is directed toward understanding causes and the effects they produce. While much remains to be learned, man has progressed far in learning the laws of nature, discovering the order of our universe, and determining the relationships between cause and effect. Many men see the hand of God behind the laws, the order and the relationships, but modern men recognize that all men are affected equally by the laws of nature. If a good man and a bad man, a rich man and a poor man, a genius and an idiot all defy the law of gravity by stepping off the top of the Empire State building, they will meet the same end on the street below. If a fetus finds its bio-chemical environment toxic and injurious to its developing cells it makes no difference if the mother is saint or sinner, brilliant or dull, wealthy or impoverished. Nature's laws will work the same for all. The same cause will be followed by the same effect. When a car traveling 70 miles per hour strikes a bridge abutment, the force of the impact will be exactly the same if the occupants are on the way to church or are on the way to rob a bank. If this were not so, there would be no law and order in nature. Some people feel this law and order is one of God's greatest gifts to man.

A father once told me that his faith in God was renewed and his acceptance of his mentally retarded child strengthened when he was introduced to the idea that God works in lawful and orderly ways. He said, "My wife and I lost our religion when we learned our boy was severely retarded. Our minister tried to tell us that God has a plan for everyone and we should pray for an understanding of what God wanted Mark to do. We tried, but as Mark got older we saw that Mark wouldn't be able to do much except perhaps through his helplessness, arouse feelings of compassion in other people. Was this to be Mark's mission—arousing compassion, we wondered? We found it harder and harder to accept our minister's point of view that God has a mission for everyone and that we should devote our lives to helping Mark fulfill his mission. More and more we began to doubt that God had any influence on us. It seemed that everything was the result of an accident. All any of us could do would be to avoid accidents."

"One night when we were sitting around drinking beer and batting the breeze we got to talking about religion and God. A fellow said he didn't understand the Bible story that man began with Adam and Eve in the Garden of Eden. He said it made more sense to think of an orderly development of man from a simple one-celled organism. He said that certain laws governed the evolution of man such as the law of the survival of the fittest animals. He asked, 'If you can't believe the Adam and Eve story, how can you believe any of the Bible? How can you believe there's a God?' Another guy asked him, 'What's behind this orderly development of man you talked about and where do these laws come from that govern nature?' They got into a long argument but I got to thinking that God must be behind the law and order of nature. Man's job is to figure out what the laws are and what the order is. When we have done that maybe we can keep children like Mark from being mentally retarded. I talked with my wife about this idea and we liked it. We saw Mark's problem as the result of man's failure to understand the laws of nature and now we think there will be many more children like Mark until man has learned to control nature better. We think it's God's plan that men will learn to control nature. God didn't tell men how to control yellow fever. He gave them the intelligence and curiosity to figure it out. It will be the same with mental retardation. I believe now that God is behind everything but He works through nature and men. This belief makes it much easier for me to understand and accept Mark and his difficulty."

This belief that in our time God works through men has provided spiritual strength for many parents. One evening the parents of handicapped children who were the members of a discussion group began talking about what they asked for when they prayed.

"I pray every day," the mother of a young cerebral palsied boy said, "and I ask God to make my boy be normal. At night I pray by my bed and I ask that I will find that Peter can walk when he gets awake in the morning. His brothers and his sister all pray for the same thing every night before they go to bed. I have faith that God will hear our prayers and Peter will be all right some day."

Another mother added, "We all pray like that, too, and I ask all my friends to pray for Allen. We are saving our money to take him to a shrine where we can all pray for him. Some day the Holy Spirit will enter Allen and he won't be paralyzed any more."

"You're praying for a miracle," another mother commented. "I think the miracle of today is the way doctors and therapists use the intelligence God has given them. I used to pray that God would make Mary all right until one day I asked myself, 'If God wanted to answer my prayer directly, why doesn't He answer all prayers directly.' I'm sure most parents of crippled children pray for their children. I asked myself why God should answer my prayers and not pay any attention to the prayers of others. My husband and I talked about this and decided that we should ask God for the ability to understand and the strength to accept Mary's problem. This helped our feelings a lot. Now we can study and talk and learn about her problems. Before we were just waiting for a miracle to happen. We think that if we want Mary to improve, we have got to give God every chance to work through those people who do His healing work today. And another thing, we ask only that the doctors and therapists help her improve in her walking and everything else. We don't expect that they can make her completely normal."

Faith is such a highly personal thing that it is difficult for anyone to know exactly what others believe and how their beliefs affect their peace of mind. It is easier to observe how one's professed beliefs influence his behavior. On this point I know of no scientific investigations, but it is my impression that those parents who are praying for and hoping for a miracle in which God will make their child normal are, as a group, less objective about their child's problems. Also, they often seem to be less careful in carrying out the instructions of physicians, therapists, and other professional workers. "After all," they seem to say to themselves, "God will take this problem away someday so these treatments aren't very important." On the other hand, parents who believe that, in our time, God works through man, tend to be more concerned about following the recommendations of professional specialists. They feel that improvement will come in their children's conditions through the combined efforts of professional workers and parents. Many of these parents have said they ask God to guide the mind and hand of the doctors, therapists, and other professional workers to whom they entrust their children's welfare. A prayer often voiced by people with this point of view—both professional workers and parents—goes something like this:

> *God, give us the ability to change what can be changed, the strength to accept what cannot be changed, and the wisdom to know the difference.*

At a professional meeting a few years ago it was my assignment to talk about the problems of parents of handicapped children. I talked about the common problems parents have discussed with me and described the ways many parents have faced their problems and found peace of mind. During the discussion period, a clergyman who was a member of the group challenged my approach to the problems of parents of handicapped children and suggested that instead of trying to trace the development of problems from common beginnings, I would do better to encourage parents to think more about the souls of their children. He believed, as I understood him, that there are souls of different sizes and a handicapped person might be blessed with a very large soul whereas a so-called normal person might have only a very small soul. It is the obligation of man and especially that of parents, he argued, to help handicapped children develop their souls to the greatest possible extent. When someone in the group asked him how one would go about developing the soul of a handicapped child and in what way having parents learn to understand the origin and development of their psychological problems would interfere with the development of their children's souls, he replied, "If we have to neglect the body to save the soul, we should neglect the body."

I have discussed this point of view many times with clergymen of different faiths and with parents and I am not clear about what he meant. Of this I am certain, however; believing in and following the recommendations of professional workers need not be incompatible with a family's developing a rich, rewarding spiritual life. I have known many parents of severely handicapped children who have conscientiously followed every recommendation and tried to carry out every instruction given by the professional workers caring for their children. They have told me that it was only the strength of their spiritual lives which sustained them when the professionals have said, "We can do no more." Their children were still dependent. The entire family of a blind, retarded, adolescent cerebral palsied boy I know derives deep spiritual satisfaction from seeing him participate in the communion service of his church, yet they have not left one thing undone which scientifically trained people have advised. Today, science can do no more and these parents have the spiritual strength to accept without bitterness or complaint the problems they face. They have changed what could be changed, found the strength to accept what could not be changed, and are wise enough to know the difference.

Several points emerge from this discussion of the relation of parental beliefs to their peace of mind and to the influence of parental faith on the kind of treatment handicapped children receive:

1. Parental religious beliefs can have a definite influence on their child's habilitation program.

Since parents come from different backgrounds and have

different training and experience, it is to be expected that a group of parents of handicapped children would represent a wide variety of religious beliefs and practices. The faith of some fathers and mothers actually won't allow a child to be treated since the parents interpret their creed to mean that if God had wanted the child to be different, He would have made him different. Some other parents so strongly hope for and pray for a miracle in which their child will be made whole that they cannot allow themselves to become effectively active in an habilitation program because such activity would weaken their faith in God's eventual healing of their child. There are many other points of view which in one way or another sometimes interfere with a child's habilitation. Greater peace of mind and more effective cooperation between parents and professional workers seem to come from the point of view that, in our time, God works through the trained, professional people in habilitating children. When failures occur it is because man has not yet learned enough about the God-given law and order of the universe.

2. Parental religious beliefs should not be permitted to interfere with a handicapped child's right to habilitative services.

Non-interference with religious worship is one of the most cherished rights of free men. It is a right which our culture would insist be preserved. However, to interpret one's religious creed as meaning that a child born with a cleft palate cannot have his palate reconstructed, or a cerebral palsied child cannot be given physical therapy, for example, is to abuse one's freedom of worship. No one, in a free society, can ever possess the right to interfere with the rights of others. In every generation handicapped persons are entitled to the very best habilitative services available in their day. No one, for religious or any other reason, should be permitted to deprive them of this right. The days of sacrificing children are past and denying a child needed habilitative services might well be regarded as a form of sacrifice to parents' concept of God's will. In the best interest of their handicapped children parents should reconsider any interpretation of their religious creed which seems to prohibit habilitative services for their children.

3. Parents should not allow their religious beliefs to interfere with the carrying out of their personal responsibilities.

When parents pray for a miracle and then hesitate to cooperate in a program recommended by professional workers for the habilitation of their handicapped child because such cooperation would show weakness in their faith, they are not meeting their obligations to their child. The same is true of parents who have deep faith that God will eventually make their child normal; hence, it is not necessary for them to carry out a program designed by man. There is truth in the old adage: "God helps those who help themselves." This belief, as Dr. Youngs points out, is made in the parable of the dishonest steward which suggests that men would suffer less if they had foresight as well as faith, realism as well as idealism, and industriousness as well as spirituality. "Very often," says Dr. Youngs, "good people suffer because they have no prudence to go with their prayers." In the case of caring for a handicapped child, prudence consists of carrying out the recommendations and instructions of qualified professional workers. The expression—"Faith conquers all"—does not mean that putting one's faith in God absolves one of all responsibility. While the Godly preface their meals with a grace thanking God for the food, they return to their labors without which the food would not be forthcoming. So it is with the habilitation of handicapped children.

Parents might pray for divine assistance and render thanks to God for the aid He has given them but they should quickly return to the labors which will bring about improvement in their child's condition.

4. Their religious commitment fills many of the needs of parents of handicapped children.

As has been explained, some religious beliefs and practices interfere with the habilitation of handicapped children. This is not to suggest, however, that the author has found no parents benefiting from their religious convictions. Some parents see divine planning in the law and order of nature and believe that man is destined to use his God-given intelligence to understand this law and order and eventually control cause and effect relationships. They see their child's handicap as a result of man's failure to understand nature and they have faith that as man's knowledge and skill increase he will be better able to prevent handicaps and to habilitate those who do become handicapped in some way. Those parents who pray for the wisdom to understand and the strength to accept their handicapped children's problems seem to open their minds to receive information about their children and they seem to grow stronger in their ability to accept the difficulties they and their handicapped children must face. From this type of prayer many derive deep and lasting comfort.

Any religion contributes to lasting peace of mind when, in it, troubled people find the strength and wisdom needed to understand and solve their problems instead of using their religion as a refuge into which they merely escape temporarily from their troubles. To help their clergymen learn more about ministering to troubled people, many seminaries have included in their training programs a study of the principles and techniques of pastoral counseling. In addition to pursuing courses dealing with problems of human adjustment, student clergymen work directly with troubled people such as those who have become patients of mental hospitals or inmates of prisons. Clergymen and lay churchmen recognize the profound influence religion can exert on the lives of people whose thoughts and feelings are troubled. There is a growing awareness that this influence can be even more effective when a pastoral counseling approach is added to the spiritual approach. This in no way detracts from the clergyman's role as a spiritual leader and advisor. Rather, it increases his ability to make religion more meaningful for troubled persons and assists him in helping troubled persons find peace of mind.

X

Those Professional People

Several years ago I presented a paper titled, "Some Ways in Which Physicians Influence the Attitudes of Parents," at a convention of professional workers particularly interested in the problems of handicapped children. The general objective of the paper was much like that of this book—to show that the problems of parents of handicapped children have their origins in common feelings and reactions and that the development of the problems follows predictable courses. As in this book, it was pointed out that when parents understand the genesis and developmental pattern of their feelings and attitudes they can control them more effectively. The paper went on to suggest that sometimes professional workers unwittingly say or do things which cause parents to be emotionally upset and to behave ineffectively. The story was told, for example, of how a physician had told the mother of a retarded child that her son would never walk. When, at 5 years of age, he did walk, the mother concluded that she and God had "outsmarted the medical profession" and, as described earlier, the physician's unwarranted prediction contributed to the development of an unwholesome attitude toward all professional workers which not only affected the lives of this family but also had far reaching effects in the community. The way in which physicians unknowingly arouse a certain type of parental guilt feeling by their questions and comments was described, and so on. During the discussion period following the presentation of the paper a prominent pediatrician ended his remarks with the comment, "The speaker has held up a mirror to our profession. He has suggested that physicians might become more aware of the influence their behavior and remarks have on the development of parental attitudes."

Professional Workers Are Sometimes Misunderstood

At the close of the session, a writer from one of the city's large newspapers which has a wide national distribution asked if he could check a couple of quotes with me. He read my statement about the physician's unwarranted prediction that the mentally retarded child would never walk and played up the use of the word "unwarranted" to mean that the physician was guilty of malpractice. He had taken the pediatrician's comments to mean that the physicians present agreed that they did not know how to treat their patients. When I insisted that he was not correctly reflecting the content of my paper he insisted that he was quoting my comments accurately because he had taken them in shorthand. When I argued that he was distorting the meaning of the remarks by quoting them out of context, he accused me of interfering with the freedom of the press. He said, "I caught the doctors with their pants down this time and, boy, I'm going to let them have it!" Nothing we could say had any influence on him because he was determined to write his story in a sensational manner. We were worried because of its possible detrimental effect on the attitudes of parents across the country so we arranged for an executive staff member of the National Society for Crippled Children and Adults to talk with the reporter's city editor who said he could do nothing about the story. He did arrange for the NSCCA staff member to talk with the reporter. She found that the by-lined story was written under the sensational headline, "Doctors Admit They Mistreat Parents." Not until he learned that the NSCCA staff member was not a doctor would the reporter listen to her point that his story, as written, would arouse much parental anxiety and hostility by making parents feel that their doctors were not treating them properly. The important facts, she pointed out, were that the doctors included a paper about parents' feelings in their session and their interest in learning more about helping parents of handicapped children develop wholesome feelings and attitudes. The story was rewritten under the headline, "Doctors Interested in the Feelings of Parents."

Professional Workers Sometimes Distress Parents

Several points are to be made from this story. First, there is in many of us a latent hostility toward professional people. The butt of many funny stories is the psychiatrist or psychologist who, in trying to help someone else, reveals his own inadequacies. Probably everyone has chuckled at yarns in which the "crazy" man betters the psychiatrist, or the psychologist is out-witted by a child. In these stories the professional people are cast in much the same role as the city-slicker who is surpassed in cunning by the farmer—or his daughter. As was mentioned earlier, when parents of handicapped children meet in small groups for counseling, it may be predicted that an early topic of discussion will be their feelings toward professional workers, particularly those with whom they first discussed their child's problem. There are many reasons why people have hidden hostilities toward professional people and it is not our purpose to try to analyze this situation thoroughly, but rather to con-sider some of the reasons why parents of handicapped children might very naturally have some hostility toward "profession-als" lying dormant, ready to spring to life on the slightest pro-vocation.

Bad News Creates Resentment

In Chapter II, "Learning Something Is Wrong," a mother was quoted as saying, ". . . I'll bet some of us would even hate the Almighty if He'd be the One to tell us the bad news." In ancient times the bearer of glad tidings was feted while the bearer of ill tidings was shunned. It's the same today. Our joy at receiving good news engenders warm, friendly feelings for the messenger. Just so, our sorrow at receiving unfavorable news can create an attitude of resentment toward its unfortu-nate bearer. Only people skilled in controlling their emotions can prevent this transfer of attitude from occurring. A doctor's announcement—"It's a boy!"—brings forth paternal smiles, a warm handshake, and the offer of a cigar. A doctor's explana-tion that a child is in some way handicapped is met with the glum silence and solemn departure characteristic of the behavior of people who are deeply hurt. Even though it is unrecognized, some of this feeling spills over onto the doctor and a seed of hostility is sown. For parents who have received bad news from a doctor to read, "Doctors Admit They Mistreat Parents," would naturally cause the seed of hostility to burst into a blooming plant. It's human nature to want to see hurt those who, even unintentionally, have hurt us. The noble practice of turning the other cheek must be learned, whereas the more primitive reaction of an eye for an eye seems to be instinctive.

Waiting Is Annoying

Another factor which often leads to the development of hostility toward professional people is the time spent waiting to see them. With physicians particularly, the amount of time parents spend waiting often far exceeds the actual amount of time spent with the doctor. The trapped position in which physicians find themselves is illustrated by the experience of a well-known pediatrician who specialized in problems of handicapped children. Doctors from all over the country referred patients to him and he had just recently recovered from a serious illness caused by overwork. Despite this, he still maintained a grueling schedule in an attempt to see everyone who needed his help. He had no way of knowing how much time he needed with each patient. Some were found to have problems which were quickly diagnosed while others required more study. In order to use his time efficiently in serving handicapped persons, his waiting room was kept full. One day a mother became more and more irate as she waited and when she was eventually shown into the doctor's office she angrily told him that he had no right to keep people waiting and that he should hold rigidly to a set schedule so people would know when they should come and when they could leave.

He answered, "Thank you for reminding me that I often forget about the time and get a way off schedule. I'll get you out of here quickly so I can see those other people."

"Oh, no, doctor," she interrupted hurriedly. "That won't be necessary. Please take all the time you need!"

This mother's reaction is typical of many. No one likes to sit and wait and when the waiting period is filled with anxiety it is especially trying. So the doctor is caught in a dilemma. Each patient wants the doctor to hurry with all the other patients but make haste slowly when his own problem is being diagnosed and treated.

Doctors' Haste Irritates Parents

A sore spot for many parents of handicapped children is what seems to them the short amount of time the doctor spends examining their child and talking with them about his problem. The extent to which some parents are irritated by the doctor's seemingly hurried attention is seen in the comments of a father who was participating in a series of group counseling sessions.

"I took a morning away from my work to go with Ned and his mother to the clinic," he said. "We were told to be there at nine and it was eleven o'clock before we got in to see the doctor. He watched us walk across the room, asked how things were going, turned and said something to the therapist, and that was all. We weren't in there more than three minutes. I was so mad that I had to concentrate on holding my hands tight against my sides so I wouldn't punch the s.o.b. Who does he think he is, anyway, to treat people like that?"

"I've felt that way many times," another father joined in. "You wait and wait and suddenly you're in and out so fast that when you're walking out you almost feel that you might meet yourself walking in. I know doctors are very busy these days but it makes you mad to be rushed around like that. It makes you wonder if it's worth going to the clinic at all when the doctor doesn't spend any more than a couple of minutes with you."

This discussion went on with various members of the group describing how their vexation had been aroused by the doctor's haste. After each had an opportunity to express himself, I asked Ned's father, "How many times has the doctor seen you and Ned?"

"Quite a few times," he replied. "I guess we have seen him three or four times a year for the past five or six years."

"Has he ever spent more than a couple of minutes with you?" I asked.

After thinking for a moment about this question, he replied, "Yes, at first he spent more time examining Ned and talking with us but lately he doesn't give us any time at all."

Another parent picked it up with, "He probably doesn't need to spend so much time now. If you've seen him three or four times a year for several years he probably knows Ned's problem backwards and forwards. Maybe all he needs to do now is make a quick check to see how things are coming."

"Well, maybe," Ned's father reluctantly agreed. "But I don't see how he can tell anything in a couple of minutes," he countered.

"I wondered about that, too," said the mother of a cerebral palsied boy. "One Saturday when we were scheduled for the doctor's clinic I thought I just couldn't make it. My husband was away, I wasn't feeling well, and I wanted to get the house cleaned up because my husband was bringing his mother back with him. I finally got myself pulled together and went. We waited and waited and then the doctor saw me for only a couple of minutes. I was as mad as a wet hen. When I took Billy in for his physical therapy the next week I jumped all over the therapist. I asked her why she'd scheduled me for the clinic when it looked to me as if the doctor didn't want to see me. 'After all,' I said, 'I wasn't in there more than two or three minutes.' She told me that the doctor could tell from the way Billy walked across the floor that he needed a special kind of lift on his right shoe. The doctor told the therapist what Billy needed and also dictated his recommendation into a special machine they have. The therapist said the doctor had about twenty more cases to see after he saw Billy and that some of them had problems which would require more time. She said that if I had missed the clinic Billy would have had to wait about three more months before he could get the lift on his shoe. I think the problem is not so much that the doctor doesn't spend enough time with us as it is that they don't explain enough to us about what they're doing. I told the therapist that, too, and she said she didn't like to tell me ahead of time what she wanted to ask the doctor or what problem she needed help with because it is better to see what the doctor thinks about it before talking things over with the parents."

"I suppose we ought to be glad our clinic has a doctor with enough experience that he can decide quickly what our children need," said another mother of a cerebral palsied child.

The parents all agreed that theirs was a "good" doctor but

some of them felt he should give them more time at the clinics. Enough parents mention being annoyed by what they regard as hurried treatment that this factor must be recognized by both parents and professional workers as a potential source of hostile feelings. Well-trained and experienced professional workers spend sufficient time with each patient to determine what kind of treatment is indicated at that time. Knowing that the child is to be enrolled in a treatment program, they may not, in the interest of seeing more children, try to get the whole picture at once. By seeing a child for several short periods over a period of several months and discussing his development with therapists and teachers the physician or psychologist can often get a better picture of the child's problems than can be obtained in one longer examination. When a professional worker finds that he needs more information about the child's problem than he can obtain in the short time available at a clinic, he will refer the family to a facility such as a hospital or university clinic for more detailed studies. All professional workers who see handicapped children and their families at clinics are aware that many parents would like to have more time to talk over their problems with the doctors. The reason why they don't receive this attention is often a matter of simple arithmetic. When the total amount of time available is divided by the total number of patients to be seen, the amount of time available for each appointment is small. Some clinics try to get around this problem by using social workers or other trained personnel to interpret the clinic's findings and recommendations to the parents. Unfortunately, many clinics cannot afford to employ additional personnel and often those whose budget would permit adding a social worker to the staff find themselves stymied by the lack of qualified personnel.

There seems to be no quick solution to the clinic problem of giving parents the amount of time they want to talk with the specialists. The feelings of many parents have been relieved when the parents realized that their children were receiving a high level professional service even when the appointment seemed hurried. With this realization comes less likelihood of a parent's taking as a personal affront the schedule-induced problem of short appointments.

Some Parents Want More Information

The oft-heard complaint that professional people never tell them anything is another basis for the hostile feelings which some parents naturally develop toward professional people.

"He treats me like I'm a child or something," said the mother of a handicapped child speaking of her doctor. "When I ask him a question," she continued, "he answers as if he doesn't expect me to understand. He acts like I should be glad he condescends to tell me anything. Sometimes I go home so mad that I wonder why I didn't slap him."

In some parents this desire to know "everything" is uncontrollable. At one clinic I had seen several times a boy whose cerebral palsy was mild but whose intellectual development was so retarded that we could predict that he would not be eligible for the regular school program. At each clinic visit I tired to help the mother develop some understanding of her son's intellectual limitations. She was so defensive and resistant that I was proceeding very slowly in guiding her interpretation of her son's developmental rate, his behavior, etc. At one clinic I had two student observers who, with her approval, sat in on my conference with her. At the close of our conference with her, I walked to the door and chatted for a moment about this and that. Later that day I learned that she had tiptoed back to the slightly opened door and eavesdropped as I explained to the students that, while all the clinical and laboratory evidence showed that her son's primary problem was mental retardation, his mother was insisting that his only problem was his poor speech. She overheard me discuss some of the possible reasons why she could not accept a diagnosis of mental retardation and listened as I explained our plan to help her understand her son's problem by using our speech therapy sessions to guide her observations and interpretations of her son's development. She then rushed to an officer of the Crippled Children's Society to complain that I was maligning her and her son. So strong was her desire to know all that the staff thought about her son that she arranged for a matron at the treatment center to "borrow" from the file the clinic's confidential records on her son. What did she gain from her eavesdropping and from her unauthorized reading of clinic reports? Nothing. In fact, she lost because she got information for which she was not ready. She rejected the diagnosis of the staff and reacted bitterly to the staff and consultants. Even though her son's development of the past several years has confirmed the diagnosis of mental retardation she cannot accept it. Further, she is so hostile to the professional workers at the clinic that they cannot establish an effective counseling relationship with her. Had she not interfered with the staff's plan to help her develop insight little by little into the nature of her son's handicap and the problems of parental adjustment to such problems, she would have greater peace of mind today.

At the other extreme are those parents who apparently hope to leave everything to the professional workers and seem to make no effort to learn about their child's problem. When, after a clinic visit, they are asked if they have any questions, their reply is something like this: "No, we figure you know what to do so we're leaving everything up to you." Often I have said to these parents, "Perhaps we could be of more help to you if we knew a little more about what you understand of your child's problem. Can you tell me what his problem is as you understand it?" Frequently, their replies reveal only a very vague comprehension of the nature of their child's problem or the plan of treatment proposed by the clinic staff. Not all this lack of information can be attributed to the reticence of professional workers for these parental reactions are sometimes found even at clinics where special efforts are made to keep parents informed and to get them personally involved in the habilitation program. And even today there are children who get to clinics only because of the intercession of a minister, social worker, relative, or other interested person. It would appear that their parents could hardly care less about them.

Information May Be Withheld Temporarily
In between these extremes, professional workers find a variety of parental reactions. Considerable training, skill, and experience are required before one can decide what information a specific parent needs, what information he is ready for, and how the information can be given most effectively. Often professional workers consider it better to have parents feel they are "not told anything" than to run the risk of giving parents information for which they are not psychologically ready. In many cases, what appears to the parents to be an unwillingness on the part of the professional worker to give more information is really the deliberate postponement of a discussion

until certain tentative conclusions can be verified or until the parental receptivity has been increased through guidance at the clinic and treatment center. Often the most effective guidance is so subtle that it escaped parental notice. Obviously, the purpose of clinic counseling would be defeated if the professional staff announced, "Our objective during your next several clinic visits is to make you ready to receive a pessimistic opinion about your child's eventual progress." So, when parents complain that they aren't told anything, this may well be true. Perhaps it is the purpose of the professional staff to help the parents make the diagnosis of their child's problem rather than for the parents to be told what the problem is. This is especially likely to be true when the professional workers suspect that the parents might be resistive to the diagnosis. Parental insistence that they be given all the facts even if the news is bad cannot be taken as an indication of parental readiness for a full interpretation of the child's problems.

Patients Sometimes Misinterpret the Diagnosis

It is not unusual for patients to misinterpret what they have been told by professional workers. Sometimes the mininterpretations are of no serious consequence but occasionally they result in unnecessary emotional distress. A number of years ago I explained to a college student our findings that her hearing loss would be handicapping in certain situations and our recommendation that she learn to use a hearing aid. She was given another appointment for early the next week. Within hours, however, we had a call from the Dean of Women asking if we couldn't see the young lady at once. It developed that she had told the girls in her dormitory that she would never be able to hear "the calls of the birds, the babbling of a

brook, or the rain on a roof." She persuaded several of them
to accompany her to the quiet of her church where she asked
them to pray for her. Alarmed, they had reported her behavior to the Dean of Women who had then called us. Her emotional reaction was far out of proportion to the seriousness of
her hearing impairment. Here is one of the reasons why professional workers must be so careful about what information
they give patients and how they give it.

Parents May Read Things Into Casual Comments

Parents will sometimes read things into the most casual comments of professional workers. One time I was asked to evaluate a 10-year-old boy whose parents were quite anxious to en-
roll him in school. On several occasions he had been admitted
to first grade but, after a few weeks, it became obvious that he
was not ready for school so his parents were advised to keep
him at home. Several tests indicated that his level of mental
development was comparable to that of the average 4-year-
old. It was clear that he was not ready for school and, in fact,
would never be ready for the regular public school academic
program. His mother countered my attempt to explain her
son's intellectual limitations by showing me an enlargement of
a snapshot taken several years earlier of her son, standing
on the shore, looking out at the ocean. She said a psychiatrist
had told her to show this photograph to anyone who suggested
that her son might be mentally retarded. She quoted the psychiatrist as advising her to ask how a mentally retarded person could look at the sea with such an intelligent expression on
his face. I later talked with the psychiatrist who remembered
the comment he made when the mother had shown him their
vacation snapshots. Instead of suggesting that the picture

showed her son to be of normal intelligence he had merely re-marked, "He's a nice looking boy. From this picture you wouldn't know that there is anything wrong with him." This was all the mother needed to have the picture enlarged as support for her insistence that her boy was not mentally retarded. The psychiatrist had another interesting picture which he had discussed with the parents. They apparently had forgotten about—or chosen not to tell me about—the pneumoencephalo-gram (air X-ray of the brain) which showed under-development of their son's frontal lobes.

Some Problems Are Difficult to Explain

Still another reason why it sometimes seems to parents that professional workers are withholding information is that the problems of handicapped children are exceedingly complex. Physicians, psychologists, and therapists spend years studying the various handicapping conditions and their treatment. Naturally, when they try to explain in a few minutes what it has taken them years to understand, and when they try to use laymen's language to describe what they have been thinking about in technical language, some things will remain unsaid. Some highly competent professional workers who can communicate fully with other professional workers find it very difficult to explain problems to parents in terms which the parents can understand. Ideally, of course, this should not be true. Every professional worker should be skilled in interpreting his findings and recommendations to parents but such is not the case. Just as a mother might know how to make a beautiful dress but be unable to tell another mother how she did it, or a father might be able to overhaul the motor of his lawn mower but not be able to explain the procedure to his neighbor, so it is that a professional worker might competently examine and treat a handicapped child but not do a good job of communicating to the parents about the child's problem. The complexities of the problems are so great that one cannot explain them completely to someone who has not studied how to make a dress, overhaul a motor, or diagnose and treat the problems of handicapped children.

Yes, as the experience with the news reporter reminded us, parents of handicapped children very naturally have some hostile feelings toward professional people. It is difficult to have only warm, friendly feelings toward those who spend only a little time with you after keeping you waiting a long time, who seem to give you only meager information, and who often give you bad news about a loved one. Human nature being what it is, a little resentment is bound to appear in some parents of handicapped children. Unless its presence is recognized and its causes understood this resentment can develop into feelings of hostility toward professional workers, thus creating a barrier to a handicapped child's progress.

A second point about professional people was emphasized by our experience with the news reporter. Suppose he had published his article under the heading, "Doctors Admit They Mistreat Parents." Would this statement necessarily be true? No, it wouldn't. This eye-catching headline would contain two misleading implications. First, the headline suggests that doctors actually mistreat parents and somehow they were caught at it and, second, the doctors admitted their wrongdoing. The convention speech on which the reporter based his article carried no charge of mistreatment. To describe some ways in which physicians and other professional workers influence the attitudes of parents is far different from accusing them of malpractice. Let us suppose that a number of physicians have been prescribing a new drug for their patients and one of them discovers and reports at a professional meeting that this drug sometimes produces an undesirable effect on certain patients. Would you say that because of this undesirable reaction of certain patients to the drug the doctors using the drug were guilty of mistreating their patients? Hardly. No more should one accuse doctors of mistreating parents because a speaker at a professional meeting reports that sometimes the comments and advice of professional workers produce undesirable emotional reactions in the parents of handicapped children. The use of the word "mistreat" in the original headline obviously did not represent accurately what was said. Likewise the words "doctors admit" misrepresent what took place. Only one doctor rose to discuss the paper. He was speaking *to* rather than *for* the other physicians present when he said that the previous speaker, by describing the reactions of parents and quoting their comments, had held up a mirror in which the doctors might study the effects of their management of the problems of handicapped children and their parents.

Through this analysis parents can see the potential danger to their peace of mind that lies in uncritical reading of sensationally written news or feature stories. In this case the headline, "Doctors Admit They Mistreat Parents," would play upon the naturally present, but usually latent, parental hostility toward professional people. Dropped into the fertile soil of latent hostility, this seed of doubt about the adequacy of one's treatment could grow until it constituted a formidable psychological barrier between the handicapped child and his parents on one side and the professional workers on the other side.

A number of years ago we saw the harmful effect of sensational reporting. We had taught a middle-aged woman to talk again after her larynx had been removed because of a malignant growth. There was nothing new about our teaching her to swallow air and then regurgitate it to produce speech sounds. In fact, this was an old procedure which had long been used by clinics both in this country and abroad. What made her case newsworthy was that her husband had a hearing loss and could not understand the faintly whispered speech which was all she could produce after her operation. For months they had communicated by writing notes to each other. Now since she could speak loudly again and he had been fitted with a hearing aid, they could talk to each other again. The public relations department of our university prepared a factually correct news release which it sent to newspapers in our area. This story of a family rehabilitation held such human interest that a wire service picked it up. Not wanting to publish what he referred to as a "university news handout," an enterprising reporter for a large city paper called me by phone for more information. He also called our patient who by then had returned to her home. I was aghast when I read his story, for it was headlined, "Penn State Clinic Invents New Voice Box." Even though most of the story was factual, I realized that the headline and his use of terms such as "miracle-workers" would create problems for many handicapped persons.

Immediately we began getting hopeful letters and phone calls from laryngectomized patients or their relatives. They wanted to come to Penn State to be fitted with our new voice box. Months later we were still receiving letters from persons whose hopes had been raised by news of our "invention." As I explained that we had no new invention—that it was merely an unfortunate use of words in a news headline—I was troubled about the inevitable feeling of discouragement my letter would bring to a laryngectomized person and his family.

Parents Can Learn to Read Critically

Today there is an ever-increasing number of articles appearing in newspapers and magazines dealing with topics which, until recently, were discussed only in professional journals. So common now are such articles that doctors refer jokingly to one popular digest as "that eminent medical journal." Doctors joke among themselves about having to keep up with the popular magizines so they will know at least as much about modern medical developments as their patients do. Psychologists, educators, and other professional workers are finding the public becoming more and more informed about professional matters. There is much about this trend that is good and desirable. In fact, it is only when the public is misinformed or when an article stimulates false hopes or generates undesirable emotional reactions that professional workers object to the reporting of professional topics in the popular press.

Parents can learn to detect falseness or exaggeration in stories about professional news. Through their training and ethics, professional workers are taught to be modest in their claims. They subject new techniques to searching analyses before announcing them and then they report on their work through professional channels rather than via public communication media. As a rule, professional workers shun publicity because it interferes with their work and, since most scientific developments result from the labors of many people, they feel that personal publicity is often unfair to one's professional colleagues. To assist newsmen prepare accurate reports of scientific developments, many professional organizations maintain press offices and require speakers to supply abstracts of their papers for release to the press. These abstracts are written in the careful language of the clinician or investigator. Any sensationalism will usually be the contribution of some writer's trying to catch the public eye.

Where do parents of handicapped children get their image of professional workers? There are probably three main sources: their own personal contacts with professional workers, comments of other people about their contacts with professional workers, and stories in newspapers and magazines. The way some parents say *those* doctors, or *those* psychologists, or *those* therapists, or *those* teachers suggests that the image is not always that of highly trained persons devoted to serving their fellow man to the best of their ability. Many factors operate to obscure this image; yet, this basic interest in helping others is characteristic of professionals, regardless of specialty, who work in the fields of rehabilitation of handicapped persons. Even when the professional keeps you waiting, tells you less than you think he should, or appears to rush you through your appointment, or irritates you in some other way, his basic interest is in helping you with your problem. If this were not so, he probably would be earning his living in some other way.

XI

A Positive Action Program

Several years ago the director of a program for which I am a consultant made an appointment for me to talk with the parents of one of the cerebral palsied children enrolled in the school. This 10-year-old boy had received treatment for several years at a treatment center in his home area. Not satisfied with the progress he was making, his parents wanted him to have a trial of intensive therapy and education and so he was accepted in our program on an experimental basis. It was apparent at the end of his first semester with us that he had made little progress. Largely because his parents had so little understanding of their son's problems he was continued in the program for another semester and efforts were made to help his parents understand that in addition to his motor handicap, their son's rate of intellectual development made formal academic training inadvisable. They rejected this diagnosis and insisted that he could get along in school very well if we would teach him to speak better. At the end of the second semester it was the consensus of the entire staff that the boy had reached the feasible upper limit of treatability and educability. The predictable amount to be gained by further intensive treatment would be too small to justify further enrollment in the school. Since his parents continued to insist that his only problem was his poor speech, arrangements were made for me to have a conference with them.

Knowing that they had driven some distance, I greeted them and said, "You certainly had a beautiful day for your trip. How long did it take?" The father told me and I asked, "Was there much traffic?"

He started to reply but his wife snapped, "That's not what we came here to talk about! What about Robert?"

Taken aback a little, I said, "Yes, we're all very much concerned about Robert, aren't we? Our entire staff has studied Robert very carefully during the past year and his speech therapist has worked very conscientiously with him. I've been wanting to ask you if you've noticed any improvement in his speech."

"Oh, my yes!" she replied.

I waited a moment and when she didn't continue I asked, "In what way is his speech better now than it was a year ago?"

"He tries harder," she answered.

"Do you think strangers can understand him any better now than they could, say a year ago?" I asked.

"I guess not," she admitted reluctantly. "But that's your job. You're supposed to teach him to talk better," she went on with growing agitation.

I then tried to explain that the cause of his speech problem was twofold. He had difficulty controlling the muscles used in speaking and his level of intellectual development limited his responsiveness to speech therapy. I explained in detail the kind and amount of speech therapy we had given Robert and concluded, "Our records show that he hasn't made any real progress."

"Your records! Your records!" Robert's mother exploded. "Why, I wouldn't trust doctors or therapists to decide if a child has made any progress. The only one who can tell if a child has made any progress is the child himself!"

While I was thinking about this, the father asked, "Are you trying to tell us that Robert can't return to this school next term?"

I explained the process by which each child in the school is evaluated periodically by the staff and told them that, in our opinion, we had tried everything we knew how to do for Robert. "The entire staff agrees," I said, "that Robert has not sufficient potential for improvement to warrant our accepting him for next term."

The father replied angrily, "I'm an officer of our local crippled children's group and our board of directors would never let any doctor or therapist decide that a child should no longer be treated. We'd treat them all. If we had too many kids we'd raffle off another Cadillac and add another room to our building and hire more therapists and get more doctors if we needed them."

I learned later that Robert's father was active not only in his local crippled children's group but in the state group as well. Someone rather perceptively observed that this family needed a handicapped child. Without it, they would have gone unrecognized in their community. As parents of a handicapped child, they had achieved a community status which would otherwise have been unattainable for them. Partly through the efforts of these parents their community had constructed a fine building for treating handicapped children. Unfortunately, however, the program was not as impressive as the building. The community rehabilitation services available to handicapped persons and their families left much to be desired. The activities of Robert's parents could hardly be expected to lead to the development of an adequate community program for handicapped persons because they were operating without a properly conceived and evaluated philosophy. As we have seen, their efforts in behalf of handicapped persons had brought them no closer to an understanding and acceptance of their own family's problems. These parents had never worked through their early feelings of confusion, yet they were trying to provide guidance for others.

Unfortunately the guidance followed by many communities in programming for handicapped persons is no better than that provided by Robert's parents. Parents of handicapped children have an obligation to see that their community's planning for handicapped persons is sound. As citizens of a democracy, they, of course, are concerned about careful and effective community programming in all areas. As parents of handicapped children they have a special responsibility to work toward the development of adequate services for handicapped persons.

Action at Two Levels Helps Parents

Several times it has been pointed out that parents of handicapped children find participation in a two-level positive action program an effective antidote for their troubled feelings. The first level is a personal level. Working at this level parents provide for their own handicapped child all the examinations, treatment, special education, and other services recommended by the staff taking care of him.

The second level is broader in perspective. When working at this level parents are concerned with developing programs designed to improve the welfare of all handicapped persons. It has been suggested that when parents concentrate all their efforts at the first level they develop a narrow view of their child's problem. However, when parents also participate thoughtfully in projects organized in the interest of all handicapped children they develop increased understanding of their children's problems. They also find through judicious participation at this second level greater personal peace of mind. There is still another reason for parents to become active at this second level. Obviously, it will not be possible for a family to obtain all the services they and their handicapped child need if these services are not available. Unfortunately, this is often the case in communities throughout the country today. The properly guided assistance of interested parents is often necessary in developing adequate community services and facilities for handicapped persons. "But," you might protest, "this is not true of our community. We have an organization for crippled children, an organization for cerebral palsied children, an organization for mentally retarded children, and so on." I am sure you could tick off the names of several more groups in your community, as could the parents in many of the communities in our land today. In your community, however, as in all the other communities, you will find it difficult, if not impossible, to obtain a comprehensive program for a handicapped person and his family. Why is this so?

Community Conscience Is Easily Satisfied

It is very popular today to be interested in the handicapped. The conscience of every community demands that something be done to help those persons who are less fortunate than their neighbors. This, of course, is a highly desirable attitude for a community to hold. Unfortunately, however, the community's drive to do good is usually satisfied before the needs of the handicapped are fully met. This leads to the development of partial programs which are often harmful to the handicapped person and dangerous to the community. They are harmful to the handicapped person because, since he doesn't get all the help he needs, he does not make optimal progress. Partial programs are dangerous to the community because they lead to an attitude of complacency. When citizens contribute to a fund drive, they usually feel no additional responsibility to the cause for which the money was raised. When a board of directors can point to the insignia of its agency on the front of a building, the directors too often feel that they have adequately discharged their responsibility to the persons their agency was created to help. How can it be different? As we have pointed out many times, rehabilitation is a complex process. What citizen, what director can know enough about it to guarantee the development of a comprehensive program? In some communities agencies employ an executive director but not one in a dozen has any training in the field of rehabilitation. To add a few professional people to the board does not ensure adequate guidance for the program because they are too busy to devote enough time to know what is going on and often they, too, are unfamiliar with the essentials of a comprehensive rehabilitation program. Far too often, then, rehabilitation programs satisfy the need of the community to "do good," but they don't satisfy the needs of the handicapped persons whom they were organized to serve.

Program Should Meet Needs

Everyone would agree that the nature and extent of the program a community develops for its handicapped should be determined by the needs of the handicapped person living in the community rather than by the desire of the citizens to be of help. A community program should be organized on the philosophy that *every* handicapped person, regardless of type of handicapping condition, age, race, or creed, is entitled to *all* the rehabilitation services which are required to meet his needs and which will lead to a maximum utilization of his potentials. An adequate community program must recognize that the family and not just the handicapped individual requires attention and would include at least the following services:

1. Early identification of the handicapped individual.

Generally speaking, the sooner a rehabilitation program is begun, the better the handicapped person's chances are for achieving maximal rehabilitation. In the case of children, treatment should be initiated as soon as it is discovered that something is wrong. The very important early years are sometimes lost because a child's problem was not discovered soon enough or he was not referred early enough for rehabilitation services.

2. Thorough evaluation by an appropriate team of professional workers.

Rehabilitation is too complex a problem for any one specialty or profession to handle alone. Handicapped persons need thorough medical examinations often including special studies, psycho-social evaluations, educational and vocational studies, etc. Careful coordination of the efforts of these professional workers and an integration of their findings are essential in establishing a complete description of the handicapped person's problem.

3. All necessary treatment indicated by the results of the evaluation.

Obviously, it makes poor sense to give the handicapped only part of the treatment which his evaluation showed to be necessary. Nor is it sensible to give him treatments which are not recommended simply because they are available. Medical and surgical care; physical, occupational, and speech therapy; and other treatment services must be provided as needed. Again, careful coordination of these services is essential.

4. Appropriate social and welfare programs.

Handicapped persons and their families need help in learning to understand, accept, and work effectively at solving their problems. Psychological counseling is needed to prevent the development of mal-attitudes and emotional disturbances and to eliminate those which have developed. Rehabilitation is costly and many families need financial assistance from welfare agencies.

5. Appropriate educational programs.

Handicapping conditions often make it difficult if not impossible for persons to participate in those educational programs which have been designed for non-handicapped children. Special educational programs designed to meet their unique educational and physical problems must be provided for them.

184

The adult handicapped sometimes need re-education which can be provided only through special programming.

6. *Appropriate vocational programs.*

Self-sufficiency is the goal of all individuals and the handicapped often achieve this only through special vocational training and employment in specially designed workshops. Even when self-sufficiency is not attainable some simple type of sheltered employment leads to improved mental hygiene for the handicapped person and his family.

7. *Appropriate recreational programs.*

Recreation is now recognized and accepted as an essential part of normal living. Whenever possible, the handicapped should be included in the normal recreational activities of families and communities. Sometimes, especially with the severely handicapped, this is not possible. Then special camping programs, swimming programs, and other activities especially arranged for the handicapped must be provided by the community.

8. *Public education and information programs.*

Two of the major problems of the handicapped are public disinterest and public misunderstanding. Public disinterest leads to failure on the part of a community to provide necessary rehabilitation services. Public misunderstanding leads to social rejection of the handicapped, withdrawal of vocational opportunities, etc. The lot of the handicapped person will improve as the public learns more about the kinds of problems he has and what can be done about them. Without the active interest and understanding of the public no rehabilitation efforts can be successful.

9. *Support of professional training programs.*

There are not enough physicians, therapists, teachers, psychologists, social workers, and other personnel to provide the services needed by handicapped persons. The community must give financial support to recruitment of new personnel and in-service-training programs for present personnel. New techniques and philosophies are developing rapidly in all fields of rehabilitation so, to be optimally effective, rehabilitation workers must be continually studying. Support of scholarship programs, financial support for attendance at professional meetings, etc., is necessary to develop and maintain a supply of qualified personnel.

10. Support of research programs.

That we don't know all about the diseases or other factors which result in handicapping conditions is obvious. Nor do we know all about how to treat handicapping conditions once they develop. Intensive study of these problems will eventually lead to more effective methods of helping those who do become handicapped. The public has a responsibility to provide funds to support such studies. Money invested in research will, in the long run, pay higher dividends in the form of better services to handicapped people than will the same amount of money invested in direct services. For this reason volunteer health agencies should ear-mark a certain portion of their annual funds for the support of research.

11. Development of those facilities which are necessary for the care of the handicapped.

Full use of existing facilities should be made through the co-operation of all community agencies interested in the handicapped. Continuing thoughtfulness must be exercised to avoid the duplication of facilities and personnel which is not only costly in terms of time and money but, even worse, often results in a fractionating of the handicapped individual with several agencies clamoring for their share. Where needed facilities are not available, the community should plan to develop them or work with other communities to develop them.

This is what handicapped persons need and what they have a right to expect of their communities. A comprehensive program of the type suggested here cannot be developed under the leadership of people like Robert's parents. I sat one time in a meeting of a community development committee which was reviewing agency requests for financial support and heard a director of a local crippled children's society boast that he had saved the community five thousand dollars a year by vetoing his agency's hiring of a physical therapist. Considering that there was nowhere in his county a physical therapist available for treating crippled children, his veto was hardly the action of a man committed to providing for *all* the needs of handicapped children. Yet, this man was a board member for over 15 years! One can say almost categorically that it is impossible for a completely local agency with no state or national affiliations to develop a comprehensive program for handicapped persons. A completely local program would of necessity be a direct service program only. The organization and carrying on of professional training programs and research activities require the combined efforts of many communities. Large scale projects of these types can best be handled by the combining of communities into state and national groups. Recreation programs, public education programs, development of needed facilities can usually be done best through the joint efforts of communities acting through a central office. Despite this, I heard an officer of a local crippled children's group proclaim that his society would affiliate with the state group only over his dead body. This man, a respected member of his community, held membership on the board of that local crippled children's society for more than 20 years and his society has not yet affiliated with the state group.

Parents Have a Role in Programming

You might ask, "What does all this have to do with the feelings and attitudes of parents of handicapped children?" There are two important ways in which a parent's philosophy of rehabilitation and his concept of an adequate rehabilitation program affect his feelings and attitudes.

First, parents are sometimes inclined to feel that only those aspects of a treatment program from which they benefit directly are important. With this point of view, they see the primary purpose of fund raising as that of providing for the operating costs of a program consisting primarily of diagnosing and treating the problems of individual children. The expenditure of money for examinations; braces and other types of medical care; speech, occupational, and physical therapy; and for those administrative costs essential to providing these services is easily understood and accepted. When, however, parents find that money is being requested for activities which, as they see it, are of less direct benefit to their children, they sometimes feel that the requests should not be approved. A father once remarked to me that when the local agency sent a contribution to the state and national groups with which it was affiliated, it was "short changing" local handicapped children. He felt hostile toward the board of directors for spending its funds so "foolishly." "Why should we support a bunch of bureaucrats when we can make better use of the money in our own community?" he argued. It's very easy to become so concerned about the personal problems associated with having a handicapped child that one's point of view is narrowed. This father could see that when communities pooled their resources for highway construction, better roads for all resulted. He could understand that, left to themselves, communities would not be able to develop uniformly high quality public school programs.

As we talked, he conceded that in almost every area we can think of, broad problems can be attacked more effectively when communities work cooperatively with other communities. In the center where his child was treated this father had access to many booklets dealing with problems of handicapped children. His community, working alone, would not have produced these booklets but, by contributing to its national agency, it had helped make these booklets possible. At a statewide meeting the therapists of his treatment center had spent two days studying recent developments in the treatment of handicapped children. Again, no independent community can conduct in-service training for its staff. There are too few staff members to make a local training program feasible. Instead of "short changing" its handicapped children, the contribution of the local group to the state organization had helped provide better trained and more interested therapists for the children. Suppose that parents and other local persons had insisted that every cent collected in The March of Dimes be retained for local use. We would not now be on the threshold of eliminating polio. This crippler is being brought under control through research supported by local contributions to a national organization. Some central administration is necessary if many local communities are to work together effectively. To charge the personnel of central administrations with being "bureaucrats" is to react emotionally rather than rationally. Today many persons have an almost automatic negative reaction to any kind of centralization of power. This view needs re-examination as it relates to programming for rehabilitation programs. Affiliation with state and national programs does not mean surrendering control of community functions to a central agency. What it does mean is the joining of forces with others in order to carry out responsibilities to the handicapped which one community cannot carry out alone. Understanding of a modern concept of rehabilitation such as described here will provide parents with a basis for reacting rationally rather than emotionally to questions involving the use of funds raised for rehabilitation of handicapped persons.

Second, a parent's philosophy of rehabilitation and his concept of an adequate rehabilitation program affects his feelings and attitudes. It gives direction to his efforts in behalf of handicapped persons. Many professional workers question the advisability of encouraging parents of handicapped children to participate in the planning and direction of programs for handicapped children. Parents are too emotionally involved, they argue, to think objectively about matters of policy formulation and administration. Often this is true. Robert's parents are a case in point, and many other parents are, in varying degrees, like them. They have no broad concept of a community's responsibility to its handicapped. They think only of providing more and more direct services. They detract from the quality of service offered their handicapped children by interfering with professional responsibilities and activities. They see themselves as missionaries and are driven to wage crusades for poorly conceived causes. They lack the knowledge and perspective needed to guide the orderly and sound development of a comprehensive program for handicapped children. This is how many professional workers have seen the parents who became directors of organizations concerned with the problems of handicapped children—and they are often right! There are such parents.

One must ask, though, how objective was the man who "saved" the county five thousand dollars a year by vetoing the employment of a physical therapist. He was not the parent of a handicapped child. He was the top administrator of one of the community's largest businesses. What about the man who vowed that his local crippled children's society would affiliate with state and national agencies only over his dead body? He was not the parent of a handicapped child. For years he had earned his livelihood in positions to which he had been elected by the citizens of his county. I have heard of meetings of boards where members approached the analysis of the crippled children's society's annual report as if they were studying the profit and loss statement of their corporations. One man divided the total operating cost by the total number of treatments given and proposed that during the next year, the executive director concentrate on finding ways to reduce the cost per treatment below the figure he obtained. He never exhibited any interest in finding out what kinds of people were being treated or of what the treatments consisted. He was concerned only that the program cost too much for the number of people being served. Obviously, this "intellectual" approach is no better qualification for membership on a board concerned with the solving of problems of handicapped children than the "emotional" approach of parents.

Informed Parents Can Serve Effectively

Parents of handicapped children, more than any other citizens, have a social responsiblilty to see that *all* needed services are available to *all* handicapped persons. They can carry out this responsibility only if they understand, accept, and follow a philosophy of rehabilitation which transcends their concerns about their personal problems. With the perspective that comes from a sound philosophy of rehabilitation and an understanding of their own feelings, parents can develop the detachment from their personal problems which is necessary if their endeavors in behalf of the handicapped are to be effective. Their concern for the welfare of handicapped persons growing out of their own personal experiences can provide a drive which, when properly directed, can produce broad benefits for handicapped persons. Our communities need the help which informed, well-adjusted parents can provide and there are many capacities in which parents can be of service. Some of the most effective board members I have observed have been parents of handicapped children. They were effective not because they were parents of handicapped children but because, as parents of handicapped children, they had been motivated to learn how to work effectively in the interest of all handicapped children. They used both their heads and their hearts, never letting one completely dominate the other. This is not to suggest, however, that boards concerned with problems of handicapped children should be comprised only, or even predominately, of parents of handicapped children. Our point is that board membership should not be denied parents of handicapped children simply because they are parents of handicapped children and that properly qualified parents should not hesitate to accept board membership. Most boards would be strengthened by the membership of at least one well-informed, well-adjusted parent.

Many Groups Only Help Parents Escape Their Problems

There are many committees and organizations through which parents can work to bring about needed legislation, more adequate facilities, and improved services. One which has a great potential for producing results is the parents' council. In many communities the organized efforts of parents of handicapped children have been the moving force behind the development of essential programs. Unfortunately, not all parent groups are so successful. Many groups seem to operate to help parents escape their problems rather than to help them face and work through their difficulties. I once heard a parent group spend an entire evening arguing about whether they needed both a recording and a corresponding secretary. On another occasion I listened while a group wasted its time trying to decide whether it should have more white or more dark cakes for its bake sale, and at another meeting a lengthy discussion centered around the kinds of aprons they should make for a fund raising project. There was no clear purpose for which the funds were to be raised but the parents all felt that the best way to help handicapped children was to raise money. Many parent groups are started with high hopes but, after floundering around for a few months, attendance drops and the organization disintegrates. Those groups which are most successful seem to serve a threefold function. First, they help parents become informed about handicapped persons and about programming for their rehabilitation. Second, they provide a medium through which parents can carry on a variety of activities in the interest of handicapped persons. Third, they provide a setting in which parents can make friends and socialize with other parents of handicapped children.

———

Does participation in a two-level positive action program mean that parents of handicapped children should devote their entire lives to their handicapped child and the broader problems of rehabilitation? Absolutely not! Many thoughtful people feel that the greatest tragedy in having a handicapped child occurs when parents withdraw from everything but those activities directly related to their children's problems. Recently I saw the young parents of a 3-year-old mentally retarded, cerebral palsied boy. They were an attractive and talented couple. She was a licensed dental hygienist, had played the cello in her community orchestra, taught a Sunday School class, and was active in the League of Women Voters. He was a graduate engineer, had sung in a church choir, belonged to a service club, and was active in scouting. All this changed when they learned of their son's problem. They cut themselves off from their community. Soon she gave up membership in the community orchestra and he quit the church choir. She lost interest in the League of Women Voters and he gave up scout work. When I talked with them they seemed to feel that by concentrating all their time and energy on their son they could somehow make him normal. They couldn't. Nor could professional workers ever habilitate him to a level of self-sufficiency or independence. Their concentration was on the first level activities of providing services for their son. Hopefully, they will someday participate in the second level activities which will broaden their perspective. One would hope though that they would not devote all their time, thought, and energy to problems of the handicapped. It hardly seems right to deprive the community of their musical talents or to deny the scouts and Sunday School of needed leadership. If they re-establish themselves with their choir, orchestra, clubs, etc., not only will their community benefit but, as persons, they will enjoy a richer life and a deeper feeling of self-fulfillment.

This goes for all parents. Working in the interest of handicapped persons does not require that one wear blinders to cut out awareness of everything else in the world. Singleness of purpose is not always the desirable trait it appears to be for it is often just a manifestation of narrow-mindedness. Narrowness in one's approach to life seldom leads to peace of mind. Nor does it assist one in stimulating his community to provide adequately for handicapped persons. In a real sense handicapped children make for handicapped families which, in turn, make for handicapped communities. A parent's obligations are not only to his handicapped child and to children like him but also to the community of which his family is a part. We see parents who seem to try to keep themselves so busy with outside activities that they never have time to think of their personal problems. They are as misguided as the couple which withdrew completely from its outside activities. Neither of these actions leads to peace of mind. Parents of handicapped children who have learned to understand their feelings and attitudes can maintain the perspective which enables them to meet their responsibilities to their children, to their families, to themselves, and to their communities.

At the close of this book it is appropriate to ask if a parent of a handicapped child can expect to eliminate his problems by following the two-level positive action program herein discussed. If one learns to understand the nature and developmental patterns of his feelings and attitudes, labors diligently to provide the services his child needs, and works conscientiously in the interest of all handicapped persons, will all his problems eventually disappear? No. Parents of handicapped children, like everyone else, cannot expect to get rid of all their problems. All they can do is to follow the advice of Robert Browning who wrote in *Bishop Blougram's Apology:*

> *The common problem, yours, mine, everyone's,*
> *Is—not to fancy what were fair in life*
> *Provided it could be,—but, finding first*
> *What may be, then find how to make it fair*
> *Up to our means.*